MATT CHRISTOPHER

On the Ice with....

MATT CHRISTOPHER

On the Ice with...
Wayne Gretzky

Little, Brown and Company
Boston   New York   Toronto   London

First Edition

Library of Congress Cataloging-in-Publication Data

Christopher, Matt.
    Wayne Gretzky : on the ice with — / Matt Christopher. — 1st ed.
        p.   cm.
    ISBN 0-316-13789-8 (pbk.)
    1. Gretzky, Wayne, 1961– .   2. Hockey players — Canada —
Biography. I. Title.
GV848.5.G73C57 1996
796.962'092 — dc20   96-3042

10 9 8 7 6 5 4 3 2 1

MV-NY

Published simultaneously in Canada
by Little, Brown & Company (Canada) Limited

Printed in the United States of America

To my son Duane

Contents

MATT CHRISTOPHER

On the Ice with....

Wayne Gretzky

Chapter One:
1961–70

From the Backyard Rink to Front-Page News

Wayne Gretzky grew up in Canada dreaming the same dream as generations of young boys before him. It is the winter dream of his homeland — a dream of hockey glory.

Dotted by frozen lakes, ponds, and rivers, the Canadian countryside in winter is virtually one skating rink after another. Playing hockey on those rinks is a part of many boys' lives. But from the time he could lace up his skates, Wayne made hockey more than just part of his life. It *was* his life.

Wayne Gretzky was born to Walter and Phyllis Gretzky on January 26, 1961. He was greeted by two generations of hockey fans. Walt Gretzky had grown up skating and playing hockey on the Nith River and, in his early adulthood, spent five years at the

Junior B level (roughly the equivalent of A minor league baseball in the United States).

Wayne's grandmother was also an avid sports enthusiast. A big fan of the Toronto Maple Leafs, Mary Gretzky holds a significant distinction in hockey history: she was the first goalie to defend against Wayne. Every Saturday night, while the Canadian Broadcasting Company telecast a program called *Hockey Night in Canada,* two-year-old Wayne would whack at a sponge ball with a tiny souvenir hockey stick as his grandmother sat in a reclining chair and played goalie.

Fortunately for Mary, Wayne didn't have to wait long to get out on the ice. Two months before his third birthday, Wayne tried out his first set of blades. A family film clip tells the story: equipped with a regulation-size hockey stick cut to scale, and bundled by his mother from head to toe, little Wayne took off. Shooting-practice sessions with Grandma in the living room were behind him. This Gretzky's life was destined to be spent on the ice.

At first, Wayne skated mainly on the Nith River near his grandparents' farm and at the local rink on weekends. Then Walter began to take Wayne to an outdoor park near their house in Brantford, Ontario. Wayne loved skating at the park and would stay long after all the other kids had gone home.

Walt Gretzky did all he could to encourage Wayne's love of hockey, but one winter of waiting in a freezing car at the park was enough for him. The next year, he turned his backyard into a skating rink so he could watch his son from the warmth of his own kitchen.

The "Wally Coliseum," as this homegrown rink came to be known, covered the whole Gretzky backyard and was equipped with lights. Four-year-old Wayne skated constantly: before school, after school, and after dinner. The rink soon became the centerpiece of all neighborhood activity.

Playing with his friends was fun, but at age five Wayne asked his father when he could play on an organized team. Since at that time boys had to be at least ten years old in order to play minor (youth) hockey in Brantford, it looked as if Wayne would just have to be patient.

Then the following fall, Walt Gretzky saw a notice in the local paper. It was an announcement for an open tryout for a major novice team at the local rink. No age restrictions were given.

When Walt and Wayne arrived at the rink for the tryouts, the ice was packed with boys. Six-year-old Wayne looked tiny beside many of them, but despite his size, he was as strong a skater as any of them. When he was on the ice, the puck became his personal property — a fact that didn't escape the notice of Brantford Atoms coach Dick Martin. Coach Martin remembered him as a "scared little boy," but he liked Wayne's skating and put him on the team.

A hockey team roster usually lists eighteen skaters and two goalies. Six players take to the ice at one time. On defense are the goalie and a pair of defensemen. The goalie is responsible for keeping the puck out of the goal any way he can. He gets help from his defensemen, whose job it is to keep the opposing team from getting in good position for a shot on goal. When the defensemen get control of the puck, they clear it to their offensive front line, the center and two wings. The front line powers forward, passing the puck back and forth, carrying it down the ice into the attacking zone, and setting up chances to score.

All players can score (though it is highly unusual for the goalie to do so!). A goal can be made in three ways: a setup pass from one player is shot into the net by a second; a pass is deflected off the stick of a second player into the net; or the puck is shot directly into the net. In the first two instances, the last player to touch the puck is credited with the goal, while the player or players who helped set up the shot are awarded with an "assist." In the third situation, only the player who scored is credited, since no one assisted him in making the goal.

Personal offensive statistics list a player's number of assists and number of goals, which together make up a total number of points. Team victories are awarded two points in league standings; if a game goes into an overtime sudden death, the winning team gets one point, but the losing team is given one as well.

Wayne Gretzky scored only one goal during his first season (1967–68) at center with the Brantford Atoms, and he didn't win any trophies. But in his second year, he scored 27 goals and gained national notoriety. And at the end of the 1969–70 season, his scoring totals climbed to 104 goals and 63 assists for 167 points in only 62 games. Word on the "Gretzky kid from Brantford" began to spread.

Chapter Two:
1970–75

Troubles in the Home Arena

Skeptics played down the hockey prodigy's accomplishments, doubting that he could possibly continue such a pace as he progressed through the minor hockey system. Nine-year-old Wayne quieted most of their doubts by ending the 1970–71 season with 196 goals and 120 assists for 316 points in just 72 games.

The next year, he silenced them completely, scoring 378 in 82 games, along with 116 assists for an astonishing 494 points.

What made Wayne Gretzky such a dynamo? From the time he first began to play, he exhibited a remarkable sense of anticipation on the ice. His intuitive instincts (often referred to as "hockey sense") were astounding. He seemed to be a step ahead of everyone and everything.

He was never the fastest skater end to end but he was the quickest laterally, particularly when pouncing on a loose puck or moving to an open area. His puck handling and passing ability were incredible. His shot often wasn't the hardest, but nobody could get a shot off more quickly. He dodged defenders and passed to teammates with consistent precision.

The media attention that was to become such a regular part of Wayne Gretzky's life began during the 1970–71 season. The local paper, the *Brantford Examiner,* ran a story about Wayne and his linemates, Chris Halyk and Ron Jamula, calling them the highest-scoring line in all of hockey. Suddenly the undersized blond kid from Brantford was signing autographs and receiving fan mail!

At the close of the season, Wayne's last with the Atoms, a writer for *Canadian Magazine* came to Brantford to do a two-page feature on Wayne. The article included a Wayne Gretzky bubblegum card. While still collecting bubblegum cards himself, Wayne had the distinction of being on one!

In 1972, Wayne Gretzky was finally eligible to play in the minor hockey league he had first asked about when he was only five years old. He and his fans hoped that his great success would continue. But in his first season competing against bigger, older players, he scored only 105 goals. Even though that was a league high, the voices of his detractors rose once again.

Wayne countered by scoring 192 goals in the 1973–74 season and 90 in 1974–75. The critics were silenced.

Young Wayne Gretzky's tremendous ability and love of hockey were undeniable. But his rise to hockey stardom was so swift, he never really had time to be a kid. Few eleven-year-olds have played hockey in front of eleven thousand people or needed a police escort to get in and out of a rink. But one memorable night went a long way toward reminding him that he was just another kid with heroes like every other kid.

In 1972, Wayne's hometown hosted the Kiwanis Great Men of Sport Dinner. Among those sports celebrities at the head table were pro football quarterback Joe Theismann and Detroit Red Wings center Gordie Howe, Wayne's all-time hockey idol. Also seated at the table that night was Brantford's own hockey superstar — four-feet-nine-inch, eighty-pound Wayne Gretzky.

Upon meeting his idol, Wayne was positively awestruck. But Howe treated his young fan like one of the guys. He even offered him a piece of advice — "practice your backhand shot." Wayne has never forgotten those words.

Yet it was after dinner that Howe proved himself worthy of admiration. The dessert dishes had just been cleared when suddenly, Wayne heard himself being called up to the microphone to speak! Standing awkwardly, the tongue-tied and embarrassed eleven-year-old didn't know what to do. Without hesitation Gordie Howe got up, approached the mike, and said, "When someone has done what this kid has done in the rink, he doesn't have to say anything." The crowd erupted in applause and Wayne gratefully sat down.

If all the other adults in Wayne's life had behaved with the same kindness and understanding, Wayne's childhood might have been a lot happier. But from an early age his wondrous hockey skills carried a negative side. As Wayne's list of personal achievements grew, the parents of other talented players began to resent him. They felt their kids were being overlooked. As their frustrations mounted, they started bringing stopwatches to games, calculating Wayne's playing time, then complaining that their kids were being shortchanged.

A shy, soft-spoken boy by nature, Wayne became extremely withdrawn around adults. His upbringing had always stressed the importance of being respectful to his elders, so he didn't feel he could respond to the comments targeted at him. Those early experiences may explain why, as an adult, Wayne has always taken his responsibility as a role model to children so seriously.

In 1974, thirteen-year-old Wayne caught a glimpse of what his life could be like if he continued on the road to hockey stardom. His team, the Brantford Carcon Chargers, played in the Quebec International Pee Wee Hockey Tournament. The tournament attracted the top teams from both the United States and Canada and gave the kids the unique opportunity to play at the Colisee, then the home of the World Hockey Association's (WHA's) Quebec Nordiques.

In Brantford's first game, Wayne put in 7 goals

and 4 assists to tie a single-game scoring record set by hockey legend Guy Lafleur. The headlines of the Quebec newspapers screamed his name. Everywhere he went, Wayne was accosted by auto-graph seekers. The only way he could get around between games was to swap jackets with one of his teammates. Tickets at the fourteen-thousand-seat Colisee were becoming scarce.

Brantford advanced to the quarterfinals. Wayne needed a police escort just to get to the locker room before the game. He scored three goals (called a "hat trick"), and Brantford defeated the Verdun Maple Leafs. Though Brantford fell to Oshawa, their arch rival, in the semifinals, nothing could di-minish what Wayne had accomplished: 13 goals and 13 assists in 4 games.

After the Quebec tournament Wayne Gretzky was truly a national celebrity. Yet in his hometown, the animosity toward him was even stronger than be-fore. But it wasn't until February 2, 1975, that Wayne finally said "enough is enough."

February 2 was Brantford Day, an event of civic pride that included a youth hockey game played in a real National Hockey League arena. Fourteen-year-old Wayne and the Chargers were going to have a chance to skate at Maple Leaf Gardens in Toronto. Like the rest of the kids there, he was excited about the competition and eager to do well. But when he skated onto the ice, his excitement vanished.

Brantford natives — the same people who would later put up a sign proclaiming "Brantford, Ontario . . . Home of Wayne Gretzky" and speak of how proud they were of their town's hero — were booing and catcalling their own star player.

Chapter Three:
1975-77

The Move to Toronto

The incident at the Brantford Day game was a painful but eye-opening experience for Wayne and his family. Torn between his love of the sport and the desire to be a normal kid, Wayne became withdrawn and unhappy. Something had to change.

Then, in the spring of 1975, a solution presented itself. A friend of the Gretzkys', Sam McMaster, was in charge of an organization called the Young Nationals, a member of the Metropolitan Toronto Hockey League. He and Wayne had become friendly over the preceding two years. So when McMaster learned of Wayne's situation in Brantford, he simply offered him an opportunity to play in Toronto.

Wayne was very excited about the prospect of leaving Brantford.

For Walt and Phyllis Gretzky, it was time to make a difficult decision. They realized that if Wayne was to continue his hockey career, he couldn't do it in Brantford. They knew that Wayne could be more anonymous as both a hockey player and a person in Toronto. But how could they possibly let their son leave home at age fourteen? Toronto was sixty miles from Brantford and a big city with all the problems that big cities could present for an impressionable kid.

At first, the Gretzkys didn't think the move was in Wayne's best interests. But Wayne wouldn't let up. After a long period of consultation with his school principal, teachers, and hockey coaches, Walt and Phyllis came to the decision that Wayne was mature enough to go. That turned out to be the easy part.

Sam McMaster assured the Gretzkys that Wayne would have no trouble switching from Brantford hockey to Toronto hockey. The necessary releases were obtained. Bill Cornish, the general manager of the Toronto Nationals bantam team and later Wayne's legal guardian, would house him in Toronto. Wayne enrolled in school in Toronto. All seemed to be going smoothly.

Then the adults intruded once again.

The Ontario Minor Hockey Association (OMHA) stepped in to prevent Wayne from playing for the Nationals. The association contended that Wayne's move was made only to further his hockey career. Wayne's parents pleaded that sending their son away from home was for his overall well-being. Walt stated his disbelief that "parents couldn't send their own child to the city of their choice, have him live with the people he wanted, and do what they all wanted as a group." But their protests fell on deaf ears.

Wayne was suspended from hockey. His career was in limbo.

He had three options. He could try to appeal OMHA's decision in court, which could cost him a half season or more; play hockey with the Ontario Hockey Association (OHA) at the Junior B level in Toronto; or return to Brantford and play with his peers at the bantam level. Walt felt that the third option was the only possible one. Wayne would have to return home.

Wayne saw things differently. He refused to deal with the continued animosity in Brantford. But he wasn't interested in fighting a time-consuming court battle that would keep him from playing, either. In his mind, there was only one direction to go: OHA's Junior B. After much discussion, his parents agreed.

Suddenly fourteen-year-old Wayne, all 135 pounds of him, was going to compete against twenty-year-olds. He would be the tiny six-year-old, lost in his oversized jersey, playing with the bigger, ten-year-old boys all over again. His parents were worried. Would he be able to hold his own against the more experienced players?

In his first game for Coach Gene Popeil's Junior B squad, the Peterborough Petes, Wayne dispelled all doubts. He scored his first goal early on. With his team two men down due to penalties, he skated faster and played harder. But only after he added another goal later in a 4–2 victory did Wayne's parents breathe a sigh of relief. It appeared things would be okay, on the ice.

Through 7 games in 1975, Wayne had 5 goals and 5 assists. He was adjusting well to the faster pace played at the Junior B level. Most important, he was happy. Then the adults stepped in once again.

The governing body of the OMHA threatened to extend his suspension to the Ontario Hockey

Association (OHA) and thus prevent him from playing Junior B in Toronto. If successful, Wayne would be forced back to Brantford.

The national media across Canada pounced on the story. They were staunchly behind Wayne, supporting his choice to play where he pleased.

On December 5, 1975, some six months after the ordeal had begun, the OHA made its decision. In its opinion, Wayne was eligible to continue playing Junior B hockey for the Nationals.

While the situation was under discussion, Wayne had been sidelined for almost two months of hockey. Yet he still managed to post 27 goals and 33 assists for 60 points that first season. He was named the league's Rookie of the Year for his efforts.

Although the Gretzkys could claim an ultimate victory by eventually getting Wayne on the ice and keeping him there, they didn't succeed in removing the spotlight from their son. If anything, the media attention intensified. Throughout the hockey world, rumors abounded about money and gifts that had been paid to Wayne's family to move him to the Nationals.

There was no truth to the stories. All that Walt and

Phyllis had ever wanted was for their son to be happy. While playing Junior B for the Toronto Nationals that season, he was. Luckily, the rumors died out, leaving Wayne to do what he did best: play hockey.

The following year promised to be a vast improvement over the previous one. All the controversy was behind him. Wayne was a legal hockey player who could now simply concentrate on the game. As a tenth-grader at West Humber Collegiate he did well in school, participating in basketball and cross-country as well as hockey.

Despite his successes in previous years, early in his second season of Junior B Wayne was rated under two hundred on the Major Junior scouting evaluation list. He was still adjusting to his new environment and he battled some health problems, including a strain of mononucleosis. But as the season continued, the Gretzky name moved up the charts steadily. He finished the 1976 season fourth in league scoring with 36 goals and 36 assists for 72 points. In the playoffs, he racked up 75 points in 23 games and led the Nationals to the league title. By the time of the final evaluation Wayne was ranked as the number two overall prospect.

Members of the Major Junior A league were beginning to take a serious look at Wayne. Such attention was important for Wayne's career. The Junior A league produces most of the National Hockey League's players; those who can't cut it in Junior A rarely make it to the NHL.

Wayne Gretzky was eligible for the Junior A draft in the spring of 1977. His chances of being selected looked good. But behind all the excitement was an important consideration. Depending on the team that drafted him, Wayne, all of sixteen years old, could end up over five hundred miles away from his family.

Walt and Phyllis Gretzky had reluctantly allowed their son to move sixty miles away at age fourteen. This time they stood firm. They couldn't allow their son to move ten times farther away two years later. So Walt Gretzky wrote letters to the teams that were the farthest removed from the Toronto area stating that if drafted by one of those teams, Wayne wouldn't report to play.

Angelo Bumbacco, the general manager of the OHA Sault Sainte Marie Greyhounds, paid no attention to Walt Gretzky's letter. His hockey club, some five hundred miles away, selected Wayne with the third pick in the draft.

Walt pleaded with Bumbacco to trade Wayne's rights to a team closer to Brantford. Bumbacco flatly refused. He insisted that Wayne play hundreds of miles away from home at age sixteen.

The Gretzkys eventually visited Sault Sainte Marie, but the efforts of Bumbacco and the Greyhounds to sign Wayne on seemed for naught until Wayne met with the Bodnar family. Jim and Sylvia Bodnar had moved from Brantford to Sault Sainte Marie; their son Steve had played hockey with Wayne. When the Bodnars offered to take Wayne into their home to live, Wayne decided to sign with the Greyhounds. For the second time a good family had influenced Wayne's life in a positive way.

Wayne was ready to make the jump to Major Junior A. For the first time he could honestly think of his professional hockey dream becoming a reality. He was now one step away.

Chapter Four:
1977–78

Number 99 Is Born

Wayne Gretzky's Junior A debut was a most auspicious one. He scored 3 goals and added 3 assists for 6 points in a 6–1 win over the Oshawa Generals. His reward for being named "player of the game" was a bottle of aftershave. There was only one small problem: he hadn't begun to shave.

As a sixteen-year-old playing against the best eighteen- and nineteen-year-olds in hockey, Wayne was in a familiar position. He had always been the youngest player on his team. It was a trend that would continue throughout his early career.

It was while playing for the Greyhounds in "the Soo," as Sault Sainte Marie is familiarly known, that Wayne wore his trademark number 99 for the first time. Upon reporting to his new team, Wayne requested number 9, the number worn by his hockey idol, Gordie Howe. Unfortunately, 9 was already worn by a three-year veteran. In his first game in Junior A Wayne wore number 19, then switched to number 14. Neither number felt right.

Then a news story caught his eye. A major NHL trade shifted future Hall of Fame center Phil Esposito from the Boston Bruins to the New York Rangers. Esposito had worn number 7 for the Bruins. But the Rangers had a number 7: Rod Gilbert, a veteran and one of their most popular players. So the new Ranger center switched to number 77.

Greyhound coach Muzz MacPherson suggested Wayne do the same. Why not two nines instead of one? Wayne agreed to try out the new number. It's been his signature ever since.

Nicknamed "Pretzel" because of his hunched-over skating style, Wayne followed his opening game success with a 6-point game followed by a 7-point game early in the season. After 7 games he was the league scoring leader with 10 goals and 16 assists for 26 points. The fear that Wayne would be intimidated at the Junior A level disappeared.

Under Coach Muzz MacPherson's offense-driven

system, Wayne was a scoring machine. MacPherson let him play the role to the hilt — but not necessarily to the team's advantage. Although Wayne succeeded in breaking the old league record of 170 points, collecting 70 goals and 112 assists for a total of 182, the Greyhounds were not a good team that year. With so much emphasis placed on offense, their defensive capabilities suffered.

Critics began to question Coach MacPherson's handling of Wayne, forcing him to defend the huge amount of ice time that his prize scorer received under his system. There was grumbling among the Greyhounds as well. MacPherson did his best to eliminate the potential for controversy by meeting privately with the team; in his opinion, he told them, their youngest teammate was going to some day "set records that aren't going to be broken for a long, long time." But as the media focus on Wayne and his scoring accomplishments increased, nothing could stop the inevitable jealousies. The public couldn't get enough of Number 99, yet the team's dismal performance — and criticism of MacPherson — continued.

In the end, Coach Muzz MacPherson was unable

to resolve the tension. In February of 1978, only halfway through the season, he resigned. The new Greyhounds coach, Paul Theriault, took charge immediately. Among the changes he made were a decrease in Wayne's playing time and an increase in attention to the defense. His strategy helped turn the team around down the stretch of the 1977–78 season, though they were quickly knocked out of the playoffs.

Wayne was happy about the team's performance, but unhappy that he wasn't playing as much. With less time on the ice, his scoring totals were only good enough for second place in the league; future NHLer Bobby Smith beat him out with 192 points. Wayne also finished second to Smith for Most Valuable Player honors, though he did win the league award for most gentlemanly player, with just 14 penalty minutes for the entire season.

With the defense-minded Theriault firmly established as the Greyhounds' coach for the following year, the prospects for Wayne and his creative offensive style of play looked bleak. It became clear that remaining in the Major Junior A as a Sault Sainte Marie Greyhound would be a serious mistake for Wayne's overall future hockey development. Something had to be done.

The next logical career move was to turn professional. But as always, Wayne's age presented a barrier. The National Hockey League had developed very strict age restrictions to protect the junior hockey league. No NHL team could sign a player under twenty. As a result, junior clubs kept the star performers so vital to their financial survival and the NHL maintained the Junior A level as its own developmental farm system. This system had kept order in the hockey world since 1963.

Then, in 1971, a new rival league, the World Hockey Association (WHA), challenged the domination of the NHL.

The WHA needed star players in order to succeed. The league set out to meet this goal in two ways. One was to sign players away from existing NHL teams. The other was to sign underage Junior A players immediately. Such aggressive recruiting led to warfare between the two leagues, which continued for the next several years.

Things were starting to calm down just as Wayne Gretzky made his international hockey debut at the prestigious 1977 World Junior Hockey Tournament in Montreal, Quebec. The tourney became a showcase for the skills of a kid who would come to be called the Great One — and focused the WHA's attention to him.

In six games Wayne tallied 17 points and received All-World All-Star recognition. John Bassett, a renegade WHA team owner who had renewed the WHA-NHL war by signing superstar Ken Linseman, offered Wayne a contract to turn pro with his Birmingham team. The WHA's New England Whalers also came calling, offering a long-term deal that included a $250,000 signing bonus. The Whalers offer was of particular interest to Wayne, since his boyhood idol, Gordie Howe, played for the team.

As it happened, Wayne never had a chance to choose. Talks of ending the league rivalry by merging the WHA into the NHL had opened. The Whalers, eager for the merger to move forward, withdrew their offer to Wayne as an act of goodwill.

Wayne was free to entertain other prospects. Enter the WHA Indianapolis Racers and their owner, Nelson Skalbania.

The Racers were a losing team. Attendance at their games was extremely poor; the likelihood of their fitting into the WHA-NHL merger was slim. Skalbania realized he had nothing to lose by taking a chance on a talented, headline-catching teenager looking for a place to play.

Nelson Skalbania was a millionaire real estate developer from Vancouver, British Columbia, who longed to make a splash in the sports world. He owned or co-owned professional teams in football, baseball, soccer, and hockey. He had tried to acquire the American League's Seattle Mariners and a National Basketball Association franchise for Vancouver. Racquetball, distance running, and backgammon were among his favorite hobbies. He was a man accustomed to getting what he wanted.

When Skalbania met the seventeen-year-old Gretzky and his family in June 1978, it was evident that he meant business. He sent his private jet to Toronto to fly Wayne, Walt, and Phyllis to Vancouver. At the airport, his Rolls-Royce was waiting to drive Wayne to his mansion. After greeting Wayne, Skalbania took him on a six-mile run. It was Skalbania's own personal physical fitness evaluation.

Wayne used his old cross-country training to beat the millionaire.

Skalbania's advisers had told him Wayne was an exceptional player, but Skalbania admitted that he had never seen him play. For him, hockey was strictly business. What was important to him was the fact that signing Wayne could give his team a better position in a future NHL merger. Because the WHA was interested in strengthening its overall position, too, the organization agreed that Skalbania should sign Gretzky.

Although officials of the WHA had made up their minds, Wayne still had a tough decision in front of him. He could sign on with the Racers, but if the two leagues merged before his twentieth birthday, the age limit would extend to him again. He would be left with no option but to return to junior hockey.

He decided to risk it. All that was left was to work out the contract details. The circumstances regarding that process were as strange as all the other aspects surrounding the situation.

Skalbania owned the Indianapolis Racers, but he was also negotiating to buy either the Houston or Quebec WHA franchises. He honestly didn't know which team to put Wayne on once he signed him.

It was Wayne himself who came up with the solution. On board the plane en route to Edmonton to make the announcement that he was joining the WHA, the seventeen-year-old wrote out his own contract.

It was not a standard agreement between a player and a team. It was a "personal services" contract between Wayne and Nelson Skalbania. Though Wayne would start out as an Indianapolis Racer, the clause left Skalbania free to move Wayne to any of his other teams. The terms of the contract factored out to $825,000 over four years, with an option to renegotiate in three years. The deal included a $250,000 signing bonus.

When questioned about what would happen if the NHL merger occurred and Wayne wasn't allowed to play, millionaire Skalbania had a humorous reply. "I guess I've bought myself the world's most expensive racquetball partner," he observed.

On his arrival in Edmonton, the media circus surrounding Wayne was as wild as it had ever been.

Wayne wasn't intimidated. After all, he had been doing interviews since age eight.

After the formal announcement of the signing, Wayne and his parents got back on the plane, bound for Indianapolis. Walt asked Wayne one final time if he was absolutely sure about his decision to turn pro. Wayne said he was sure. Wayne was now a Racer. His journey to the pinnacle of his sport was just beginning.

Chapter Five:
1978

A Dream Come True

The doubts that had hounded Wayne every step of his career didn't end when he turned professional. NHL writers and broadcasters openly questioned his decision to go pro. At five feet eleven inches and 164 pounds, Wayne was far from an imposing physical presence. But as had been pointed out by his first coach, Dick Martin, Wayne looked small only until he took control of the puck. Then everyone on the opposing team looked scared.

The summer before his pro hockey debut was a relaxing one. Wayne worked on his skating and played a lot of baseball, a sport he had always loved. Then, on September 11, 1978, exactly three months after signing his personal services contract with Nelson Skalbania, Wayne Gretzky began his first professional training camp.

Wayne got along well with his first pro coach, Whitey Stapleton, a former standout NHL defenseman. If anything, Stapleton seemed overly protective of his young phenom. What Stapleton and most adults didn't realize was that Wayne had been playing under intense pressure for years. He was used to it. For the fourth straight year he was in a different league, at a higher level, with a new set of teammates. He was determined to give the Racers his all.

He barely got a chance. His career as a Racer lasted only eight games, during which he scored a mere 3 goals and 3 assists for 6 points. But it wasn't his hockey ability that was to blame.

It turned out that Indianapolis was simply not a hockey town. Nelson Skalbania's expenses for each game were double what the gate receipts were bringing in. Without the support of fans, no team — no matter how many good players it has — can survive for long. Before the end of the season, the struggling team folded. Wayne's Racer career was over almost before it had begun.

Desperate to recoup some of his losses, Skalbania made a logical business decision. Regrettably, Wayne Gretzky and his big salary would have to go.

Wayne was officially informed of the impending midseason trade by Coach Stapleton. He was placed in the enviable position of choosing where he would go. The choices came down to Edmonton or Winnipeg. Edmonton, an oil boomtown in Alberta, seemed like the smart choice. The franchise was solid. It was leading the WHA in attendance. The Oilers would undoubtedly join the NHL in the event of a merger.

Wayne's preference was clearly Edmonton. But suddenly, final financial questions in the negotiations between Oilers owner Peter Pocklington and Nelson Skalbania arose. As a result of these questions, the deal was held up. In fact, when Wayne boarded a plane with two other players who had been traded, their destination was still up in the air! Only after clearing customs in Minnesota did the nervous players learn where they were going: next stop would be Edmonton. The Racers were to become Oilers after all.

In order to secure Wayne's services, Peter Pocklington had paid Nelson Skalbania $850,000. He had also agreed to assume the four-year personal services contract Wayne had signed with

Skalbania less than five months earlier. Nelson Skalbania, the man who had been so instrumental in bringing Wayne to professional hockey, would soon be completely out of the game.

Wayne, still only seventeen, lived briefly with Edmonton head coach Glen Sather before settling in with Ray Bodnar and his wife. Ray was the brother of Jim Bodnar, the man who provided Wayne with a home in Sault Sainte Marie while he played for the Greyhounds the previous year.

When he took to the ice the first time with his new team, Wayne was ready to play. Unlike Indianapolis, Edmonton was a hockey town — and Number 99 was determined to conquer it. He set high goals for himself: to play a full eighty-game schedule to demonstrate his durability and to hit the 20-goal and 40-assist marks.

It took only a couple of weeks of observation for owner Peter Pocklington to realize what he had in his new center. Pocklington contacted Wayne's agent, Gus Badali, to offer Wayne a twenty-one-year deal. If accepted, Wayne would be an Edmonton Oiler until 1999, when he would be thirty-eight years old. It was basically a lifetime contract, in terms of hockey.

Pocklington had a good reason for wanting to tie the rookie star into such a deal. The NHL-WHA merger was very close. He didn't want to risk losing Wayne to an NHL team if Wayne was placed back in the draft after his twentieth birthday.

Wayne talked to his agent, carefully weighed his options, then decided to take the offer. He would earn a staggering $280,000 per year for the first nine years guaranteed, along with a $100,000 signing bonus. Following that, there were two six-year options.

The Oilers were delighted that Wayne had accepted their offer. The WHA was very happy to have the budding superstar secured in its league. An elaborate ceremony was planned to celebrate Wayne's signing.

On his eighteenth birthday, January 26, 1979, Wayne signed his Oilers contract at center ice at the Northlands Coliseum, home of the Edmonton Oilers. The house was packed, and unknown to the youngest and richest Oiler, his entire family was part of the crowd.

Some of the veteran Oilers players advised Wayne not to sign his name to such a long-term contract. But thirty-three-year-old Ace Bailey, Wayne's road roommate, told him not to listen to them. The veteran felt that the rookie should sign, then play to the best of his ability and try for a new, bigger contract in a few years. As it turned out, Ace's advice was sound. Two years later Peter Pocklington tore up the old contract and gave Wayne a new one.

Though the Oilers lost the game that followed the signing ceremony, Wayne Gretzky's dream of playing professional hockey had come true.

Chapter Six:
1978-79

The WHA Rookie

The WHA style of play matched Wayne's personal style. At 165 pounds he thrived on the fast pace. And the WHA was a cleaner game than Major Junior A. The fears that the lightweight Oiler would be a target for physical abuse in the pros turned out to be unfounded. If anything, the opposite appeared to be true.

At the junior level, every player is trying to make it to the pros any way that he can. Cheap shots directed at the other team's top offensive player are common.

At the pro level, players assume roles in order to stay in the game. Loyalty to teammates is a most important attribute to success. There are always tough guys ready to protect their team's scorers and finesse players. Throughout his career Wayne has had tough players on his side, allowing him to concentrate on playing his creative, improvisational game.

Wayne reached the goals he'd set for himself at the beginning of the season. He played the full eighty-game slate, not missing even one matchup in the transition from Indianapolis to Edmonton. His scoring totals far exceeded all expectations. He finished third in the WHA scoring race with 46 goals and 64 assists for 110 points. He also gained Rookie of the Year honors.

Unquestionably the biggest thrill of Wayne's rookie season was his selection for the WHA All-Star team. Chosen as the second-team All-Star center behind Cincinnati's Rob Ftorek (who would later coach Wayne in Los Angeles), Wayne finally had the opportunity to play on the same line with his idol, fifty-one-year-old Gordie Howe! With Wayne at center, Gordie on the right side, and Howe's twenty-three-year-old son, Mark, playing left wing, their combined ages made them the "oldest line in hockey," as Gordie pointed out.

The 1979 WHA All-Stars swept a three-game exhibition series against a Russian touring squad. But something was missing from Wayne's game. It was the only game of his career that "the Tuck," the distinctive way Gretzky wears his jersey, wasn't on display.

The Tuck has become as much of a Gretzky signature as his number 99. The origin of the Tuck dates back to Wayne's first season of organized hockey. As a six-year-old competing against ten-year-olds, Wayne was faced with the problem of wearing a jersey sized for an older boy. Every time he shot the puck, his stick caught in the billowing material. Walt tried to tuck in the whole jersey (or sweater, as hockey jerseys are most commonly referred to), but it proved to be too uncomfortable. Then it struck him. Why not tuck it in one side, his shooting side?

Thus the Tuck was born. During Wayne's entire career the Tuck has played a major role. When Nike provided the Oilers jerseys in the late 1980s, the Nike "swoosh" logo was shifted from the right side to the left side of the Edmonton sweaters, thus preserving the sanctity of Wayne's ritual. But in that 1979 WHA All-Star Game, Gordie Howe

40

stepped in and actually sewed Gretzky's jersey in place. Wayne couldn't argue with his idol, but the next game, the Tuck returned and remains to this day.

In his first playoff experience as a pro, Wayne helped lead the Oilers to a winning season of 48 wins, 30 losses, and 2 ties (48-30-2). With 98 points total, they took first place in the league and won a chance to compete in the Avco Cup championship. The WHA equivalent of the NHL Stanley Cup, the series was a best-of-seven-games. Though they played well, in the end the Oilers bowed to Winnipeg 4 games to 2. Wayne could still boast a solid postseason, notching 10 goals and 10 assists for 20 points in 13 games.

The following spring, the WHA's Avco Cup was a historical footnote. The WHA, which had existed from 1972–79 in an almost constant state of war with the established NHL, was finally merging with its rival.

Only six WHA franchises finished the final year. The Edmonton Oilers, the Winnipeg Jets, the Quebec Nordiques, and the New England Whalers were absorbed into the National Hockey League; the Cincinnati Stingers and the Birmingham Bulls folded. Despite being only eighteen years old, Wayne was allowed to remain an Edmonton Oiler, but now he was in the NHL.

Chapter Seven:

1979–80

The NHL Rookie

The NHL is currently made up of twenty-six teams, nineteen American and seven Canadian. There are two sections, the Eastern Conference and the Western Conference. The Eastern is divided into the Northeast and Atlantic Divisions; the Western into the Central and Pacific Divisions. The Edmonton Oilers are members of this last division.

The merger of the WHA and the NHL was hailed as a great move for hockey. From the Edmonton fans' standpoint it meant only one thing: a place in the big league. It took the Oilers just eleven days to sell fifteen thousand season tickets. All the Oiler fans were eager to see how their team would stack up against the best of the NHL. In particular, eyes were on their blond boy wonder, Number 99, the "Gretzky Kid."

For the fifth straight year, Wayne would be a rookie.

Many hockey experts openly stated that the tighter checking in the NHL would slow Wayne's freewheeling skating and brilliant passing. Could he stand solid against the very best competition? At eighteen, could he continue to be the prolific scoring machine he had been at every other stop?

Before the 1979–80 season began, Wayne set a personal goal for himself. Displaying no lack of confidence in his own ability, he predicted he would finish no lower than third in the NHL in scoring. He judged veteran superstars Marcel Dionne of the Los Angeles Kings and Guy Lafleur of the Montreal Canadiens as his chief competition for the Art Ross Trophy, an award given to the league high-scorer at the end of the season.

On October 10, 1979, Wayne's NHL career began. The Oilers traveled to Chicago to face the Blackhawks of the Central Division. The Blackhawks were one of the NHL's six original flagship franchises, and their Chicago Stadium home was a raucous building to play in.

Wayne openly discussed how anxious he and his

teammates were before the game. "I'll have butter-flies in my stomach when they're playing the national anthem," he said after practice the day before the match.

Despite his nervousness, it didn't take Wayne long to notch his first career point, assisting on a goal by nineteen-year-old Kevin Lowe, the Oilers' first-round draft pick the previous spring. With the Oilers trailing Chicago 2–0, Wayne passed to linemate Brett Callighen, then streaked to the front of the Blackhawks' net to create a screen in front of goalie Tony Esposito. Brett Callighen fed the puck to defenseman Kevin Lowe, who fired a shot past Esposito.

But Esposito proved to be too good for Wayne and the Oilers. Wayne had six shots on goal, none of which went in. "I used to hear stories about how good Espo was and tonight he showed me why," he told the media after the game. "I had four really good scoring chances and couldn't put the puck in the net."

Only four nights later, though, Wayne collected his first NHL goal. With about a minute left to play, the Oilers trailed the Vancouver Canucks 4 to 3.

Wayne partially fanned on his shot, but the puck somehow rolled off his stick and dribbled in to tie the game at 4–4.

Although Wayne was performing steadily through the first half of the season, the Oilers were not. Mired in or near last place, the club was reminded that this was not the WHA. For a team that had won the World Hockey Association regular season title the previous year, it was a hard adjustment period.

Though his team lagged, the only thing that slowed Wayne through the early season was a bout of tonsillitis. Even in his weakened state (at one point he lost eleven pounds), Wayne had an impressive line of 22 goals and 35 assists for 57 points at the halfway point of the season. He was fifth in the league in scoring, 26 points behind Marcel Dionne. For the second year in a row, Wayne was rewarded by being named a league All-Star.

After fifty-two games Wayne had moved into third place in scoring, racking up 84 points. Dionne's first-place lead had been cut to 15. Guy Lafleur was ahead of Wayne by 10. If Wayne was to win the Art Ross Trophy, he had to turn up the volume another notch.

As a team, the Oilers showed improvement in the second half of the season. A 9–1 defeat of Lafleur's Canadiens, the defending Stanley Cup champions, helped bolster their confidence. The final playoff spot in the Campbell Conference was suddenly within their grasp.

In a 9–2 rout of the Pittsburgh Penguins, Wayne pumped in 3 third-period goals. He now had 121 points, enough to move him into second place and within 5 points of Dionne. On April 2, 1980, at nineteen years and two months, he became the youngest player in league history to score 50 goals.

Hockey fans throughout Canada couldn't get enough of him. Even those who had once openly ridiculed him now accepted him as the greatest young player on the ice.

One town in particular welcomed him with open arms. His hometown of Brantford named him Athlete of the Year. When the Oilers traveled to nearby Toronto to play the Maple Leafs, the Garden — the same building Wayne had been booed in on Brantford Day five years earlier — was sold out. Wayne himself couldn't get enough tickets for this "homecoming" game. His brother Keith had to trade a scalper an autographed Gretzky stick for two tickets!

Wayne did not disappoint his fans. From the moment he took to the ice, he played what many later claimed was his greatest game ever. He was in absolute control, putting in 2 goals and 4 assists to lead the team to an 8-to-5 victory. His effort was enough to even him with Dionne at 133 points. More important, the win got the Oilers closer to wrapping up the sixteenth and last playoff spot in the Stanley Cup race.

The Oilers did manage to grab the final playoff spot by passing Washington by 2 points. The Stanley Cup playoffs would come to Edmonton.

As the NHL teams finished up the final battles, a more personal competition was being fought. Wayne and Marcel Dionne were neck and neck in the race for the Art Ross Trophy. Number 99 tallied 3 points with a goal and 2 assists in the Oilers' last game of the season. Dionne needed 2 points to tie Wayne for the title. Two assists later, they ended the season at 137 points each.

Yet in the end, the scoring honors went to Dionne. When the points were broken down into goals versus assists, the Los Angeles King had 53 goals to Wayne's 51. To the people making the final decision, this put Dionne ahead.

To Wayne and his family, however, it didn't make sense. The Art Ross Trophy is awarded to the player who scores the most points. If two players score the same number of points, logically the honor should be shared. Walt Gretzky wondered out loud at the decision. In his opinion, it seemed to devalue assists, the importance of which had always been stressed to young hockey players. But conflicting message or not, the decision stood firm. Wayne would just have to be content with second place.

That blow was sweetened somewhat by the two awards he *was* given. Ineligible for the league's Calder Trophy for Rookie of the Year because of his WHA experience, Wayne instead walked off with the Lady Byng Memorial Trophy, the league's sportsmanship award. He also became the only rookie to capture the Hart Memorial Trophy as the league's Most Valuable Player.

Wayne was thrilled about the commendations. "Winning the two awards is an unbelievable honor, especially being the first player to do it since Stan

Mikita," he said, referring to the Chicago Blackhawks Hall of Famer. "When I think about the kind of player [he is], I realize what a feat it is to accomplish this."

The Oilers showed grit in their first NHL Stanley Cup playoff series. Though they were swept three games to none by the number one seeded Philadelphia Flyers, the Oilers took the Flyers to overtime in Game One and double overtime in Game Three.

Their first season in the NHL was over.

At the end of 1979–80, Wayne went home to have his tonsils removed and to relax. His 51-goal, 86-assist season, his two awards, and his team's final standing had silenced the doubters about his ability to play in the NHL. And for once, he could look forward to a new season without the pressure of proving himself all over again.

Chapter Eight:
1980–81

"Truly Extraordinary"

The team that Number 99 returned to at the start of the 1980–81 season was young and strong. Solid defenseman Kevin Lowe and outstanding wings Mark Messier and Glenn Anderson had been added in 1979. An offensive defenseman, the flashy Paul Coffey, was plucked in the first-round draft for 1980. A highly skilled Finnish right wing, Jari Kurri, was taken later, as was goaltender Andy Moog. Edmonton was slowly but surely building a team of championship caliber.

Mark Messier became one of Wayne's closest friends and a most valuable player in his own right. He, too, had played briefly in Indianapolis in the old WHA. An intimidating physical force on the ice, Messier defined the term "power forward." But it was the addition of Kurri that proved to have the most direct positive effect. From the beginning there was an incredible chemistry between center Wayne Gretzky and his right wing. They always seemed to know where the other was on the ice. The Gretzky-to-Jari pass-and-shoot became a lethal combination.

The enthusiasm of youth played a significant part in the Oilers' second NHL season. The condescending attitude of the established teams in the league would soon be challenged by the Oilers' explosive on-ice offensive. Leading the way was Gretzky, now almost twenty years old. Throughout the season, he was a force to be reckoned with.

Perhaps his most dramatic achievement of the season came on March 29, 1981 — the night he broke the NHL record for most points in one season, a record that had stood firm since Phil Esposito had established it nearly a decade earlier.

Entering the game at the Pittsburgh Civic Arena, Wayne found himself tied with the former Boston Bruins' great with a total of 152 points. On his first shift of the evening, Wayne skated in alone on a clean breakaway. Later, when a Pittsburgh player was sent to the penalty box, he took a pass from

Glenn Anderson on a power play, skated along the right wing boards, dodged a check from a Pittsburgh defenseman, and moved to his favorite spot behind the net. He then slid a perfect pass to Mark Messier, who was waiting in front of the goal. Two seconds later, the puck was in the net!

Even though he had bested the home team, the Pittsburgh arena gave Wayne a standing ovation. They knew greatness when they saw it.

And Wayne wasn't finished. He assisted on goals by linemates Brett Callighen and Jari Kurri as the Oilers skated to a 5–2 win.

In the postgame press conference, Wayne couldn't temper his elation. "What a tremendous feeling," he said. "It's great anytime you break a record, but we won the hockey game and that's what we're here to do."

NHL president John Ziegler responded with glowing praise the next day. "Your accomplishments in only two years in the NHL have been truly extraordinary. It is with young players such as yourself in which the future of our great sport rests, and it quite obviously rests in very capable hands."

The 1980–81 season, Wayne's third as a pro, was

one of great personal achievement. His ending stats were amazing: 55 goals plus a record-breaking 109 assists (surpassing Bobby Orr's 102) equaled 164 points, 12 better than Esposito's 152. This time there was no doubt as to who the winner of the Art Ross Trophy for scoring champion would be. Wayne defeated Marcel Dionne by 29 points. Besides the Art Ross, Wayne received the Hart Trophy (MVP) and was selected for the first team in the All-Star Game, replacing his rival Marcel Dionne.

The Oilers' overall regular-season record showed modest improvement from their inaugural NHL campaign. Their 74 points was 5 better than 1979–80. They also moved up two playoff rungs, going into the Stanley Cup playoffs seeded fourteenth.

Still, few people were expecting the Oilers to perform well in the Stanley Cup playoffs. After all, their first opponents were four-time champs, the Montreal Canadiens.

The Oilers took the first round of games by storm. They waltzed into Montreal and won the first two games against the Canadiens, 6–3 and 3–1. Game Three was back in Edmonton.

The Oilers fans were primed for a nail-biting

Wayne Gretzky, after the 1979–80 season with the Oilers, poses here with his Hart Memorial Trophy for MVP and the Lady Byng Memorial Trophy for Sportsmanship.

Number 99 receives a high five from All-Star teammate Mark Messier after making his fourth goal in the 1983 game.

Wayne protects the puck from a Black Hawk defenseman during a 1983 playoff game. The Oilers took the game 6–3 and advanced to the Stanley Cup finals.

Teammates Wayne Gretzky and Glenn Anderson show their disappointment after losing Game One to Russia in the 1987 Canada Cup competition.

A battle for the puck between Wayne and New York Islander Denis Potvin.

The Great One, moments before springing into action.

The Stanley Cup comes home to Edmonton.

The superstar father with his wife, Janet Jones Gretzky, and one-year-old daughter, Paulina.

Wayne celebrates after scoring his record-breaking 1,851st point.

Wayne Gretzky's Year-to-Year Statistics (Regular Season Only)

Year/Team	Games Played	Goals	Assists	Points	Penalty Minutes
1978—79 Racers/Oilers	80	46	64	110	19
1979—80 Oilers	79	51	86	137	21
1980—81 Oilers	80	55	109	164	28
1981—82 Oilers	80	92	120	212	26
1982—83 Oilers	80	71	125	196	59
1983—84 Oilers	74	87	118	205	39
1984—85 Oilers	80	73	135	208	52
1985—86 Oilers	80	52	163	215	46
1986—87 Oilers	79	62	121	183	28
1987—88 Oilers	64	40	109	149	24
1988—89 Kings	78	54	114	168	26
1989—90 Kings	73	40	102	142	42
1990—91 Kings	78	41	122	163	16
1991—92 Kings	74	31	90	121	34
1992—93 Kings	45	16	49	65	6
1993—94 Kings	81	38	92	130	20
1994—95 Kings	48	11	47	58	6

Wayne Gretzky's Career Highlights

1978–79: WHA Rookie of the Year
Led WHA Playoffs in Goals and Points

1979–80: Hart Memorial Trophy and Lady Byng Memorial
Trophy
Led NHL in Assists
Tied the League in Points

1980–81: Hart Memorial Trophy and Art Ross Trophy
(League High Scorer)
Led NHL in Assists and Points

1981–82: Hart Memorial Trophy and Art Ross Trophy
Led NHL in Goals, Assists, and Points

1982–83: Hart Memorial Trophy and Art Ross Trophy
Led NHL in Goals, Assists, and Points
Led Playoffs in Assists and Points

1983–84: Hart Memorial Trophy and Art Ross Trophy
Led NHL in Goals, Assists, and Points
Led Playoffs in Assists and Points

1984–85: Hart Memorial Trophy, Art Ross Trophy, and Conn
Smythe Memorial Trophy (MVP of Playoffs)
Led NHL in Goals, Assists, and Points
Led Playoffs in Assists and Points

1985–86: Hart Memorial Trophy and Art Ross Trophy
Led NHL in Assists and Points

1986–87: Hart Memorial Trophy, Art Ross Trophy, and Conn
Smythe Memorial Trophy (MVP of Playoffs)
Led NHL in Goals, Assists, and Points
Led Playoffs in Assists and Points

1987–88: Conn Smythe Memorial Trophy
Led NHL in Assists
Led Playoffs in Assists and Points

1988–89: Hart Memorial Trophy
Led NHL in Assists

1989–90: Art Ross Trophy
Led NHL in Assists and Points

1990–91: Art Ross Trophy and Lady Byng Memorial Trophy
Led NHL in Assists and Points

1991–92: Lady Byng Memorial Trophy
Led NHL in Assists

1992–93: Led Playoffs in Goals, Assists, and Points

1993–94: Lady Byng Memorial Trophy
Led NHL in Assists and Points

Chosen for the All-Star Team 8 Times
Played on 5 Stanley Cup Championship Teams
All-Time Scoring Leader in Goals, Assists, and Points

match. In order to stay in the playoffs, the Canadiens had to win Game Three. But the Oilers, led by the offensive power of Number 99, would not be denied. Wayne scored 3 goals, 2 late in the second period. The second goal gave the Oilers a one-point lead they would not relinquish. A poor pass from Montreal forward Mark Napier turned into an easy goal for the always alert Wayne Gretzky. The Oilers ended the series with a decisive 6–2 win and moved on to face their next opponents.

The New York Islanders, the defending Cup champions, were up next. The heavily favored New York team took the first two games at home 8–2 and 6–3. Back in front of their own fans at the Northlands Coliseum, the Oilers won 5–2 in Game Three. Fans flocked to the rink for Game Four, hoping to see their boys tie things up.

Edmonton came out flying and took an early 2–0 lead on goals by Paul Coffey and Jari Kurri. Then the champion Islanders responded by putting in 3 of their own, including a goal made when an attempt to clear the puck from in front of the goal backfired. The Oilers battled back, sending the game into overtime on a goal by Brett Callighen.

But it was not to be. A shot on goal by Islander defenseman Ken Morrow glanced off the skate of Edmonton defenseman Lee Fogolin and rebounded into the net. Suddenly, the Islanders led the series 3 games to 1.

The pivotal game broke the hearts of the Oilers and their loyal fans. Not even the victory in Game Five could give them the boost they needed. The Islanders, en route to a second consecutive Stanley Cup championship, won Game Six to knock the young Oilers out.

Though they didn't make it to the finals, the team from Alberta had made their presence known. After only two years in the NHL, the hockey world knew that the Gretzky Kid had a formidable supporting cast. If the Oilers continued to play as they had been, few doubted they would give the older teams a run for their money in the 1981–82 season.

Wayne didn't have much time for a real off-season after the 1980–81 period. He had been chosen to represent his country in the Canada Cup.

An international competition originally created in 1976, the Cup pitted teams from the six best hockey countries — Canada, Czechoslovakia, Finland, Russia, Sweden, and the United States — against one another. The 1981 Canada Cup was the second one ever to be played. Canadians everywhere were confident that their team would prove victorious.

The series did in fact begin with a resounding 9–0 win for Team Canada over Finland. The powerful frontline combination of Wayne Gretzky, Buffalo Sabre Gil Perreault, and Montreal Canadien Guy Lafleur was devastating. Wayne himself racked up 2 goals and 1 assist.

In the 8–3 victory over Team USA, Number 99 racked up 2 more goals and 2 assists. This commanding win was followed by a disappointing 4–4 tie versus the Czechs. Wayne was held scoreless.

The next matchup saw Team Canada winning 4–3, but at a heavy price. Gil Perreault fractured his ankle and Wayne bruised his elbow badly when Sweden's Lars Lindgren slashed him.

Wayne recovered and came out fighting in the next game against the Russians. Team Canada won 7–3. Then they defeated the U.S. again, 4–1, and found themselves facing Russia once more in the finals.

Canada seemed ready, but the final game was a disaster. A hat trick by wingers Siergei Shepeleu and 2 goals from Igor Larionov set the Russian offense on fire. When the smoke cleared, the score was a humiliating 8–1.

Team Canada's defeat in the final against Russia sent shock waves across the country. "The last thing we wanted to do was lose so badly," a tearful Gretzky said. "Now what happened here will go on for another four years."

Chapter Nine:
1981–82

Moving Onward and Upward!

While vacationing in Florida, Wayne tried to put the devastating defeat in the Canada Cup behind him. Instead, he thought about the upcoming season and what he could do to help his team and improve his own standings. He pledged to shoot the puck instead of always looking to pass. It was a promise he kept.

In the first 14 games he made a total of 17 goals; after 34 games, the tally was 35. Fans started speculating on his chances of reaching the "50 goals in 50 games" milestone, a record set by Montreal center Maurice Richard thirty-six years earlier and tied by Mike Bossy of the Islanders the previous year.

With such a record within his grasp, Wayne was unstoppable. A 3-goal performance in Minnesota was followed by 2 goals in Calgary; 1 goal against

Vancouver; and 4 goals in Los Angeles. Suddenly Wayne was a mere 5 goals away — and he had 12 games yet to play!

Even more remarkable was the fact that in these 4 games alone Wayne contributed 9 assists. But the effort was not without its consequences. Wayne left the Los Angeles game in severe pain due to a knee injury. But at 5 goals away from tying Richard and Bossy, he was prepared to tough it out.

On December 30, 1981, the Oilers hosted the Philadelphia Flyers. Wayne's goal-scoring spree went into high gear for the game. He began with a tip-in late in the first period, then followed with a 35-foot drive. Two goals down, 3 to go for the "50 in 50" mark — and the game was still in the first period!

In the second period, he inched closer to the mark by streaking in alone and firing a 25-foot wrist shot under the crossbar. But he wasn't content to stop with a hat trick. Five minutes into the third period, he slammed in a 30-foot slap shot over the shoulder of the beleaguered Flyers' goalie. The hometown crowd went crazy.

But the game wasn't over yet. The Flyers had been scoring right alongside the Oilers. In the last moments of the game, they were trailing 6–5. In a move aimed at increasing their offensive power, they pulled their goalie and added an extra skater.

The vacant net proved to be the Flyers' downfall. With seven seconds left, Glenn Anderson set up Wayne, the highest scorer in the league. Flyer Bill Barber made a desperate dive, but the end result was inevitable. Nothing could keep Number 99 from scoring his fifth goal of the night, fiftieth of the season in 39 games. It was the fastest 50 in hockey history. In all, Wayne had 108 points, 40 better than his nearest rival.

After the game, Wayne's roommate, Kevin Lowe, confessed that at the pregame meal Wayne had commented on how good he felt that day. "There's no reason why I can't score five goals tonight," he said prophetically.

No record seemed safe with Wayne Gretzky on the loose. Two months later, on February 24, 1982, in Buffalo, Wayne surpassed Phil Esposito's single-season, 76-goal record. Late in the third period, Wayne stole the puck at the Sabre blue line and moved in to flick a wrist shot past Buffalo goalie Don Edwards. Score!

The game was stopped so Phil Esposito himself could present the record-setting puck to the Great One. But just so there wouldn't be any doubt about his having met and passed the record, Wayne scored twice more in the final minutes of the game.

And Wayne wasn't finished yet. With 5 games remaining in the regular season, Number 99 had 199 points, just one shy of the seemingly impossible 200-point milestone.

Wayne flew his parents Walt and Phyllis to Calgary for the Oilers' next game. He had been disappointed that they hadn't been in the crowd for his 5-goal game against Philadelphia. Nobody would be disappointed this time.

In the three periods of the game, Wayne got not 1 but 2 assists and 2 goals when his team was short-handed due to penalties. He hadn't just met the 200-point barrier, he had shattered it!

Wayne Gretzky's pursuit of the Richard, Esposito, and 200-point records captured the imagination of the entire hockey world. The world beyond hockey soon followed. Special press conferences were held wherever the Oilers were playing. The night Wayne broke Esposito's record, there were over three hundred members of the media on hand to cover the historic event. Wayne remembered it as the year he lost the last of what little privacy he had left. His was an instantly recognizable face, that of a real celebrity.

The rest of the Oilers were maturing along with the superstar. In the 1981–82 season, Mark Messier scored 50 goals. Defenseman Paul Coffey racked up 89 points and made the All-Star team. Glenn Anderson collected 105 points. And the "Flying Finn" Jari Kurri ended with 32 goals and 86 points. Edmonton's incredible offensive firepower had amassed 417 goals and 706 assists for a total of 1,123 points — all NHL records.

The cocky Oilers were ready to cruise into the playoffs. They were second only to the mighty Islanders.

The Oilers faced the Los Angeles Kings in the first round of the 1982 Stanley Cup playoffs. From the start, it was apparent that they weren't taking the Kings seriously. After all, the Kings had finished some 48 points behind them during the regular season.

Their overconfidence would prove their undoing.

In Game One at Edmonton, the Oilers squandered a 4–1 lead and lost by a disappointing 10–8. Wayne bailed out his team with an overtime game-winning goal in Game Two, but amazingly, the Oilers then blew a 5–0 lead in Game Three, losing 6–5 in overtime. The Oilers brought the series back to Edmonton with a 3–2 win in Game Four, but they had run out of steam. In the fifth and deciding game, the underdog Kings prevailed 7–4. The Oilers' season was over.

In the locker room a somber Wayne Gretzky spoke to the media. "This is worse than losing the Canada Cup," he said. "We took two big steps forward [this season], but unfortunately we took a giant step backward."

The newspapers turned on the team. "They Choked!" the *Edmonton Journal* headlines proclaimed. The team was described as "weak-kneed wimps" by the same people who had embraced their cocky, swashbuckling style before the playoffs began.

Wayne and the rest of the Oilers tried their best to put the disaster of the 1982 playoffs behind them. Nevertheless, it was a rough off-season in

Edmonton. Everywhere Wayne went he was re-minded of the Oilers' playoff failure.

The backlash against the team was more than just disappointment, however. Many people felt that the Oilers, most of whom were in their early twenties, were simply too cocky for their own good. Under the old NHL rules, many would have been barely out of junior hockey. In addition, many in the league felt that the Oilers were unnecessarily antagonistic toward opponents, officials, and referees. They doubted that this was the way for the team and its superstar to attain their ultimate goal: the Stanley Cup.

Wayne's dramatic personal accomplishments were in marked contrast to the performance of his team. Besides the Richard and Esposito records, he had broken his own NHL record for assists (120) and won the scoring title by 65 points, the widest margin in league history. But his team had been bounced from the playoffs in the first round. A new kind of pressure was building in Edmonton — the pressure for the Oilers to work together and win as a team.

Chapter Ten:
1982–83

"Can't Win the Big One"

In the off-season, Wayne had plenty of time to reflect on the triumphs and failures of 1981–82 and to consider how to approach the next year. The criticism that he couldn't deliver for the Oilers come playoff time was weighing heavily on him. After discussions with team management, it was agreed that Wayne's ice time would be cut from 26 to about 22 minutes per game. Forward Mark Messier, a budding superstar, would move from wing to center, thus giving the Oilers two strong and interchangeable centers. These decisions were aimed at saving Wayne's legs for the playoffs and, looking long term, at prolonging his career.

Wayne responded immediately to the changes. The 1982–83 season saw him set out on a 30-game scoring streak, a feat that earned him the prestigious

Sports Illustrated "Sportsman of the Year" accolade in December, the first hockey player so honored since Bobby Orr of the Boston Bruins in 1970. More important, the Oilers were on track toward Stanley Cup glory.

Named a first-team All-Star for the third consecutive year, Wayne celebrated with a four-goal third period in the league's annual game in Washington. His efforts earned him the All-Star MVP award for the first time.

Playing a full eighty-game schedule for the third year in a row, Wayne led the league in all three offensive categories for the second straight year, with 71 goals, 125 assists, and 196 points. The 125 assists broke his own 120 NHL mark from the previous year. Wayne became the first player in the fifty-five-year history of the NHL to win the Hart Trophy as Most Valuable Player for the fourth consecutive year.

But he knew that all the personal honors would be meaningless without a strong playoff showing.

Edmonton captured the Smythe Division with 5 fewer points (106) than the previous year. They scored 7 more goals (424) as a team but surrendered

20 more (315), the downside of their wide-open offensive style of play. The whole city was primed for playoff redemption.

The 1983 Stanley Cup playoffs opened in Edmonton with Wayne notching the winning goal in Game One of the preliminary round versus the Winnipeg Jets, an old WHA rival. Two single-goal wins followed for a 3-games-to-none sweep.

In the next round, the Smythe Division finals, the Calgary Flames provided the opposition. Since the Oilers' arrival from the WHA, the increasingly bitter Calgary-Edmonton rivalry had excited all of Alberta province. A bench-clearing brawl near the end of the regular season had only intensified the competition. This would be the first of several playoff meetings between the two clubs.

The Oilers jumped to a 3-games-to-none lead, outscoring Calgary 21 goals to 6. In Game One, Wayne was shut out, but Mark Messier tallied 4 goals in a 6–3 win. Fights broke out in Game Two, proving that the rivalry was far from friendly, but that didn't stop the Oilers from taking the win. Wayne was more effective in this second matchup, assisting on goals by Jari Kurri and Randy Gregg.

But it was Game Three that saw the Great One in peak form. He set up Paul Coffey for the Oilers' first goal. He converted a stolen puck and quick pass from Glenn Anderson into a wrist shot to the Calgary netminder's glove side for a second goal. Then he and Jari Kurri skated in a 2-on-1 break that earned his linemate an assist and himself a goal. Though a second breakaway was thwarted, Wayne tipped in a pass from Kurri for his third goal of the night. His fourth and final goal — a record-tying figure for most goals in a single playoff game — came off an easy backhand at close range. He finished the evening with a pair of assists on goals by Mark Messier.

In all, Wayne set a playoff record by earning 7 points in one game. He now owned or shared thirty NHL records.

Calgary came back to edge the Oilers 6–5, claiming Game Four at home. But the rout was on in Game Five. Edmonton scored six times on their first 21 shots on goal. They set a new Stanley Cup playoff series standard with their thirty-fourth goal in the third period on a score by Glenn Anderson with Wayne and Jari Kurri assisting. The 9–1 victory sent the Oilers on to their next opponents, Chicago, confident that their offense couldn't be beat.

In 5 games the Oilers had averaged 7 goals per game. Wayne himself was on a playoff record scoring pace. Could anybody stop them?

The Chicago Blackhawks certainly couldn't. In the first game of the Campbell Conference, Wayne scored his third playoff game winner in an 8–4 victory. The Oilers routed the Blackhawks again in Game Two, 8–2.

In Chicago for Games Three and Four, the scores were closer but the results the same. Three years after joining the NHL from the WHA, Gretzky and his gang were headed to the Stanley Cup finals. Four wins separated them from the big prize.

The New York Islanders, three-time Stanley Cup champions, stood between the Oilers and their championship dream. The aging New Yorkers had slipped to second in their division during the regular season. Their overall record was tied for sixth best in the league — 10 points behind the Oilers. It would be a contest of youthful energy versus experience.

The series opened in Edmonton before a wildly

cheering Northlands Coliseum crowd. But the cheers didn't last long. Islander goalie Billy Smith shut out Gretzky and Edmonton 2–0.

In Game Two, Billy Smith made his presence known in a different way. With 2:04 left to play, Wayne was positioned in his favorite spot behind the net. Smith kept his eye on him and, as Number 99 skated by, reached far out with his goalie stick and slashed him on the thigh. As Wayne fell to the ice, the play sped away toward the Oilers' goal.

Wayne recovered quickly but didn't join his teammates. He moved right up in front of the New York net and angrily taunted Smith. Both players raised their sticks. It looked as though a fight were about to break out.

The officials swiftly took control of the situation. Though Smith claimed he had been aiming for Wayne's stick, not his leg, he was sent to the penalty box on a slashing violation.

Despite this disadvantage, the Islanders won again, 6–3. The Oilers were now in a 2-games-to-none hole. The Stanley Cup was slowly moving out of their reach.

Back home in New York with a chance to win in

front of their own fans, the Islanders completed a four-game sweep, winning 5–1 and 4–2. Wayne had been held without a goal in the series, ending up with just 4 assists. Despite the Oilers' having shattered playoff records for assists with 26 and scoring with 38 points, the cries of "Can't win the big one" echoed loudly throughout the hockey world.

The Oilers did learn a valuable lesson at the close of the finals. When they visited the winning locker room to congratulate the Islanders, they expected to see jubilation among the victorious New York players. Instead they saw their rivals in various degrees of pain and injury. Bryan Trottier, the smooth center, nursed an injured knee. Denis Potvin, a three-time winner of the Norris Trophy as the league's best defenseman, held an ice pack to his shoulder. High-scoring left wing Mike Bossy and big-game goalie Billy Smith were bloodied, bruised, and black-eyed.

Wayne, Mark Messier, and the other Oilers looked at one another. There was barely a mark on them. They knew at that moment that the Islanders were not just more experienced at playing "big games"; they were more willing to play with everything they had.

Maybe the Oilers had gotten through Winnipeg, Calgary, and Chicago too easily; perhaps it had left them unprepared to fight hard in the final matchup. Whatever the reason, they had not been quite ready to climb the mountain toward a championship.

Chapter Eleven:
1983–84

One Step at a Time

Wayne was anxious to begin the 1983–84 season. Through four NHL seasons the Great One had set some twenty-four NHL records and shared ten others. He had won four straight MVP awards and three consecutive scoring titles. The three highest single-season point totals in NHL history all belonged to him.

Yet the Oilers had been defeated in the Stanley Cup finals. It was time for him to put aside personal goals to concentrate on the team.

He was prepared to do whatever was necessary to make it the Oilers' best year ever. He embarked on a vigorous weight-training program and reported to training camp ten pounds heavier and feeling stronger.

At twenty-two, Wayne was the official captain of

the Oilers, taking over the duties from defenseman Lee Fogolin. The Oilers and their captain were on a mission from the moment the 1983–84 season began. Anything less than a Stanley Cup championship parade would be considered a failure.

Edmonton's offense was more explosive than ever. In one 4-game stretch, the team scored 33 goals. During a 5-game winning streak, Wayne established an Oilers' record with two 8-point games: a 4-goal, 4-assist effort versus Minnesota and a 3-goal, 5-assist performance against New Jersey. Through 52 games the Oilers averaged just under 6 goals per game; Wayne amassed 61 goals and 92 assists for a total of 153 points. His linemate Jari Kurri was second in scoring — 68 points behind.

Only one team seemed capable of causing problems for the Oilers: the Islanders. Since the Stanley Cup finals, the Oilers had dropped six straight to the four-time defending champions. Every man on the Edmonton team knew that the road to the Stanley Cup ultimately led to the Islanders' Nassau Coliseum, but they just couldn't seem to earn a win against their nemesis.

Still, the season was steaming ahead at full speed.

Then the Oilers suffered a series of setbacks. First, Wayne's amazing streak of staying injury-free ended. He separated his shoulder when Los Angeles Kings forward Dave Taylor hit him from the side into the boards. Despite this injury, Wayne played through the pain. But when he suffered a second injury, this time to his left hand in a freak accident during a practice, he was forced out of the lineup for six games.

This seemed like an eternity for a player who had missed only one game in over four seasons. To make matters worse for the Oilers, Kurri was also out with an injury. Edmonton won only one game in six before both players reported back.

Fortunately, the time off the ice didn't seem to affect Wayne's playing. In his first game back versus Winnipeg, he plugged in 2 goals and 2 assists. Playing three games in four days during one stretch, he scored 10 goals, including back-to-back 4-goal games at St. Louis and Pittsburgh.

Despite missing six games and getting less ice time down the stretch, Wayne still finished the season with 87 goals, 118 assists, and 205 points. Forwards Glenn Anderson and Jari Kurri had earned 54 and 52, respectively, making the Oilers the first team in league history to boast three 50-goal scorers.

The team itself established an NHL record by scoring an amazing 446 goals. For the first time, Edmonton also finished with the league's best record: fifty-seven wins, eighteen losses, and five ties. It had been a long year for the Oilers, but now that the playoffs were about to begin, they were in a good position. Oilers coach Glen Sather rested his big guns instead of further assaulting the NHL record book.

That strategy paid off in the first round. Edmonton won a resounding 9–2 victory over the Winnipeg Jets in Game One. The Jets came fighting back in Game Two, only to have Oiler defenseman Randy Gregg win the game in overtime 5–4. An efficient 4–1 win in Game Three at Winnipeg clinched the series in a sweep.

The next series, the Smythe Division final, turned out to be a classic matchup between rivals Edmonton and Calgary. The Oilers grabbed Game One 5–2. But in Game Two they squandered a 4–1 lead and lost 6–5 in overtime.

The Oilers went to Calgary hungry and bounced

back with a pair of hard-fought victories, 3–2 and 5–3. Then in Game Five at home, the Oilers let Calgary back into the series with a 5–4 win. With Wayne and several of the other Oilers battling a flu bug, the series moved back to Calgary for Game Six. The Flames evened things up at 3 games apiece with a goal by their star, Lanny McDonald, in overtime.

In Game Seven, the Oilers looked to their star player to lead them to victory. And lead them he did. Using a combination of speed and finesse, Wayne paced the Oilers' attack with a goal and two assists in a 7–4 win.

"Everybody has a job to do and my responsibility is to put the puck in the net. I know I wasn't doing my job," Wayne said later, referring to the fact that he had only had 2 assists in the previous three games. "Jari and I sat down together and decided that if we had to go through people to get to the net, we'd do it."

With Calgary behind them, the Oilers moved on to their next opponents. In the Campbell Conference finals, the Minnesota North Stars, Norris Division champions, arrived ravaged by injuries. The Oilers took no chances.

Wayne scored the winning goals in each of the first two games in Edmonton, while fellow center Ken Linseman did the same in Games Three and Four in Minnesota. Edmonton had swept their way back to the finals. But waiting for them was their nemesis, the New York Islanders.

Chapter Twelve:
1984

Champs!

For the 1984 Islanders, who were four-time champions the rallying call had been "Drive for Five." They had had a solid regular season, totaling 104 points. Forwards Mike Bossy with 51 goals and Bryan Trottier with 111 points were still among the league's top offensive players. Defenseman Denis Potvin was still leading the defensive corps, and in the nets, Billy Smith, the game's best big-game goalie, was still the man. The New York team had the look of champions entering the Cup finals.

The experienced Islanders were favored to win their fifth consecutive Stanley Cup. But the Oilers were determined to give them a rough ride. Roger Neilson, formerly of Vancouver and Los Angeles, had joined Edmonton's coaching staff. He was instrumental in helping the Oilers prepare for the rematch of the previous year's finals. He planned an attack that emphasized Edmonton's strengths: speed, skating, and finesse.

The series opened on Long Island. Oilers center Kevin McClelland, acquired from Pittsburgh before the season primarily for his defensive ability, scored the only goal in a tight-checking 1–0 victory. A brilliant save by Grant Fuhr in the third period preserved the win.

Wayne couldn't help but feel optimistic about the series. The Oilers seemed able to anticipate the Islanders' every move well in advance.

New York responded like the great champions they were in Game Two. Clark Gillies' hat trick led the Islanders to a 6–1 victory. The series stood at one game apiece.

Wayne was now feeling some personal pressure. The Islanders and goalie Billy Smith had shut him out in 9 straight playoff games. The next 3 games would be played in Edmonton and he knew the fans would be expecting their superstar to perform.

The Oilers met the challenge with a 7–2 thrashing of the Islanders, but once again the Islanders were able to effectively defend against the Great

One. They used a shadow technique, assigning a player to follow him all over the ice whether he had the puck or not.

Frustrated, Wayne decided to make an adjustment in his game. He would try to hold the puck a little longer than normal, fight through the check before he made a pass, and thus open himself up for a possible return pass.

Less than two minutes into Game Four, the Islanders' domination of Wayne Gretzky ended. A great pass by Dave Semenko sent Wayne in alone on Billy Smith. A quick fake pulled Smith out of position. With the roar of the hometown crowd in his ears, Wayne flicked in his first goal of the series. As if to prove it was no fluke, he added a second goal in the third period. The Oilers took the game.

Edmonton now had a commanding 3-games-to-1 advantage. They were one victory away from their ultimate goal.

Wayne flew his whole family — Walt, Phyllis, brothers Keith, Glen, and Brent, and sister Kim — out to Edmonton for Game Five.

Prior to the match, Captain Gretzky made a brief speech to his teammates. He simply reminded his fellow Oilers how close they were to proving they were the best team in the league.

Nobody in the dressing room wanted to let the opportunity to win at home slip away. They took to the ice determined to win.

The first twelve-minute period passed by scoreless. Then Wayne and Jari Kurri took over. Twice Kurri set up the Oilers' captain for goals, first with a lead pass for a partial breakaway, and later with a drop pass off a 3-on-1 jump.

With the Islanders down 2–0, coach Al Arbour replaced netminder Billy Smith. At the start of the second period, the crowd could sense the tide turning in favor of their beloved Oilers.

On the power play in the opening minute of the middle period, Ken Linseman scored a goal on assists from Wayne and Charlie Huddy. Four and a half minutes later Kurri got a power play goal of his own, set up by Paul Coffey and Glenn Anderson. The Islanders trailed 4–0 after two periods.

Two goals by Islander Pat LaFontaine in the first minute of the third period turned the rout into a game again. But Oiler goaltender Andy Moog made several huge saves to frustrate the Islanders, including a spectacular stop on New York's Denis Potvin. Moog received a rousing ovation.

With less than three minutes left to play, the Islanders pulled their goalie in one last desperate attempt to create some offense momentum. Instead, the Oilers' Dave Lumley found the empty net with 28 seconds left. Final score: Oilers 5, Islanders 2.

The Islanders' reign as champions was over!

The Northlands Coliseum exploded. Balloons and streamers filled the air all the way to the rafters. Jubilant fans poured over the boards onto the ice. Wayne Gretzky, the captain of the Stanley Cup champions, held his little brother Brent in his arms as he skated around the rink. A new dynasty was just beginning.

When the Stanley Cup was wheeled onto the ice, Wayne couldn't wait to claim it. National Hockey League president John Ziegler never had the opportunity to make his presentation speech. Wayne hugged him, picked up the trophy, and held it aloft to the fans. The Oilers embarked on the long-awaited traditional winner's skate with the Cup as the players passed the prize back and forth among themselves.

In the locker room, the celebration continued. Champagne corks popped. Hugs and kisses were exchanged among the Oilers and their families. The Gretzkys were no exception. Walt and Phyllis were right in the middle of the bedlam.

All the personal triumphs, records, and awards seemed meaningless to Wayne now that this big moment had arrived. A look of pure joy covered his face underneath the sweat, tears, and champagne. He and his Oilers were now Stanley Cup champions.

Chapter Thirteen:
1984–85

Two-Timers

For Wayne and seven of his teammates the off-season celebration was cut short. Oilers coach Glen Sather was chosen to coach Team Canada in the 1984 Canada Cup. Several of the Islanders were also members of the team. Number 99 led them in scoring as Canada rebounded from their 1981 failure and reclaimed the Canada Cup.

The Oilers' focus now turned to defending their Stanley Cup championship. In the eyes of the hockey world, an unsuccessful title defense by Edmonton would make their 1984 victory look like a fluke. After all, the Islanders had won four Cups in a row. They had also won back-to-back titles in 1974–75. The Oilers had to prove they were more than a one-Cup team.

During the off-season, centerman Ken Linseman

was traded to Boston for the six-feet-two-inch two-hundred-pound left wing Mike Krushelnyski. Krushelnyski joined Wayne and Jari Kurri on the Oilers top line. The threesome clicked almost from the start of the 1984–85 season.

Fresh from their Canada Cup success, Edmonton broke from the gate fast with a fifteen-game (12-0-3) unbeaten streak. Wayne had a sixteen-game point-scoring streak of his own. Kurri racked up 18 goals. Paul Coffey led the defense in one outstanding game after another. The dynamic duo of netminders, Grant Fuhr and Andy Moog, were as solid as ever.

After 35 games Wayne was averaging 3 points per game. Then, on December 19, 1984, during game 424 of his career, he tallied his 1,000th NHL point. The Great One needed just under two minutes to accomplish the feat.

"I saw Wayne break for the net," said Mike Krushelnyski. "I started over to congratulate him and ended up following the initial shot that he hit the post with. I went after the rebound and it glanced off my skate and in."

Wayne continued to mount up the points as the

night went on. He scored his sixth shorthanded goal of the year. He set up Glenn Anderson for a power play goal. He started a play up the ice with a pass to Jari Kurri that resulted in a goal by Paul Coffey. He picked up another assist on a Dale Hunter tally, then finished the game with his second goal on a blistering 35-foot slap shot.

Two goals and 4 assists for a total of 6 points for the night; 390 goals, 625 assists, for a total of 1,005 points for the career!

While Wayne was well on his way to breaking most of his own records, expectations haunted the Oilers every step of the way. The inevitable happened. The Oilers slumped late in the season, winning just 3 games, losing 5, and tying 3. Considering that the core of the team had played in the Canada Cup, then reported to training camp in early August, it was not a surprise that they looked tired.

Even so, Edmonton closed out the regular season with the league's second best record. In the first round of playoff games against the Los Angeles Kings, the Oilers swept 3 straight, 2 in overtime and the third clinched by a Kurri empty-net goal. Wayne was held goalless, but did collect 5 assists.

The Winnipeg Jets, who had beaten the Oilers three straight times in the regular season, were their Smythe Division finals opponent. Wayne broke from his scoring slump with a pair of goals in a 4–2 win in Game One. Paul Coffey then took over Game Two with 2 goals and 3 assists for a 5–4 triumph. Another tight 5–4 battle followed in Game Three with Wayne bagging the winning goal. The fourth game turned into a rout as the Great One tied his single-game playoff record with 3 goals and 4 assists for 7 points.

In the Campbell Conference finals, the Chicago Blackhawks were humbled twice in Edmonton, 11–2 and 7–3. But back in Chicago Stadium the Hawks got even, winning 5–2 and 8–6 in Games Three and Four. Home again, the Oilers got back on track with an offensive onslaught led by Wayne Gretzky. The Oilers prevailed 10–5 in Game Five.

The series clincher was played in Chicago. Wayne assisted on all four of Kurri's goals for an 8–2 win. Wayne's 4 goals and 14 assists during the matchup set a single-series record.

But the struggle toward the Cup wasn't over yet. This year, the finals would feature a brand-new opponent.

The Philadelphia Flyers had ended their regular season with 4 points more than the second-place Oilers. So far, they had swept the New York Rangers, stopped the New York Islanders 4 games to 1, and outlasted the Quebec Nordiques 4 games to 2. They were in the Stanley Cup finals for the first time since 1975.

Both teams were geared up for a war. The first battle, in which Wayne was held without a shot on net, went to the Flyers 4–1. Edmonton responded with a hard-fought 3–1 victory in Game Two, bringing the series back to Edmonton.

Game Three turned out to be Wayne's show. Despite being shadowed continuously, he scored twice in the first two minutes. The first was a backhander on a centering pass from Jari Kurri. Then, a mere fifteen seconds later, he rerouted a brilliant pass from Paul Coffey to the short side of the Flyers' goalie.

Before the first period ended, he added a third goal with another short-side backhander. Not content with simply making a first-period hat trick — his seventh in playoff competition — he plugged in a fourth goal, to tie his own playoff record, and 2 assists. He also helped out on defense by beating out the Flyers' center in a face-off that could have tied the score in the game's last seconds. The Oilers were victorious, 6–5, and one giant step closer to winning the Cup.

But the Flyers hadn't come so far to be defeated easily. Game Four saw the Oilers in a 3–1 deficit until Wayne Gretzky took control. Showing his usual determination and concentration, he scored the game's final two goals, leading his team to a 5–3 win. The series stood at 3 games to 1. The Oilers were one game away.

Eager to win the coveted Cup in front of their own fans, the Oilers started fast and did not let up. Wayne set up Kurri for an early goal with a blind backhand pass. It was the first of 7 goals the team would earn in the first two periods. Wayne assisted on 2 more goals, first by sending the puck to Paul Coffey, who took it straight to the net, then by snapping a pass to Mike Krushelnyski in the slot. Wayne also contributed a goal of his own.

The Flyers just couldn't keep up. At the end of the night of Game Five of the Stanley Cup finals, the scoreboard read Edmonton 8, Philadelphia 3.

Mission accomplished for Wayne Gretzky and the Edmonton boys, two-time Stanley Cup champs!

Wayne achieved personal championship status as well. His 7 goals in the finals tied an NHL record, and he had broken his own playoff points record with 47. He also set a new standard for assists, with 30. As a result, Wayne captured the Conn Smythe Trophy for the Stanley Cup playoffs' Most Valuable Player, adding it to his sixth straight Hart Trophy (league MVP) and fifth Art Ross Trophy (leading scorer).

He was all of twenty-four years old.

The Oilers had twice broken a fundamental hockey convention: that an offensive-minded team couldn't win a Stanley Cup.

Chapter Fourteen:
1985–87

"The Hardest Cup We've Ever Won"

After a relaxing off-season, the 1985–86 Edmonton team came back even stronger than the year before. Wayne Gretzky might have had his best year ever. He shattered his single-season assist mark by 28, finishing with an unbelievable 163. That mark — better than 2 per game — could stand in the record books forever. Twice he had 7 assists in a single game. Even with his goal total down to 52, Wayne still broke his all-time single-season points record with 215. It was his fourth 200+ point season. He won his seventh straight Hart Trophy, sixth straight Art Ross Trophy, and seventh All-Star Game.

As a team, the Oilers scored 400+ goals for the fifth straight year. They also matched their 1983–84 regular season by regaining the league's best record with 119 points. The Stanley Cup playoffs appeared to be just a formality.

In the opening round of the 1986 playoffs, the Oilers dominated Vancouver. The Canucks were swept in 3 games by a combined score of 17–5.

The Calgary Flames and the Edmonton Oilers replayed the "Battle of Alberta" in the Smythe Division finals. The Flames shocked the Oilers in Game One, 4–1. The next four games seesawed back and forth between the two bitter rivals. Trailing 3 games to 2, the Oilers had to win the sixth game against Calgary to stay alive. They did just that: a 5–2 victory brought the series back to Edmonton for the deciding seventh game.

In that contest, the Flames played a close-checking game. The Oilers fell behind 2–0. But they rallied in the second period with a goal by Glenn Anderson on an assist by Wayne and a breakaway shot by Mark Messier to tie things up.

The combatants stood deadlocked at 2–2 into the third period. Then, with time winding down, Oilers rookie defenseman Steve Smith — pressed into service when Lee Fogolin was injured — tried to make a cross-ice pass from behind his net to defense partner Don Jackson. Instead, the puck hit goaltender Grant Fuhr on the back of the leg and dribbled into the net. That agonizing turnover gave the Flames a lead they wouldn't lose.

Wayne did his best to rally the Oilers, but Calgary netminder Mike Vernon stopped the Oilers cold. Through the game's final minutes, Vernon made several outstanding saves. When the final buzzer sounded, the score read Flames 3, Oilers 2. There would be no third consecutive Stanley Cup for Edmonton. That glory would eventually fall to the Montreal Canadiens.

Smith was inconsolable in the locker room. "The guys worked so hard, they deserved better," he said, taking full blame for the defeat. Coach Sather disagreed.

"We lost as a team," he said. "We had lots of time to come back." Many felt that the Oilers had beaten themselves by trying too hard to finesse a play rather than simply dumping the puck in when they had the chance.

As heartbreaking as the loss had been, the stunning seventh-game defeat inspired Wayne and the Oilers to buckle down for the 1986–87 season.

Coach Glen Sather helped the cause by adding highly skilled defenseman Reijo Ruotsalainen to the team. The acquisition would prove to be an important one. Ruotsalainen meshed in effectively with the Edmonton style, while taking some of the pressure off Paul Coffey. In addition, Finnish left wing Esa Tikkanen blossomed as an imposing all-around threat in only his second full season.

A highly motivated Oiler squad was clearly back on a mission during the 1986–87 season. To regain their status as Stanley Cup champions, the Oilers concentrated on playing better defensively; as a result, they allowed 26 fewer goals (284) than the previous year.

For Captain Wayne Gretzky it was another brilliant season. His 62 goals, 121 assists, and 183 points signaled the end of his astonishing four-year streak of 200+ points-per-season, but his overall statistical year suffered only in comparison with his one true competitor: himself. Quite simply, nobody could touch him.

Wayne also reached the first of his numerous career milestones on November 22, 1986, scoring his 500th goal versus Vancouver. The goal itself was a long shot lobbed into an empty net, and was just 1 of 3 he would score that night. He was particularly pleased that he reached that record in an at-home game. His 100-, 200-, 300-, and 400-goal marks had all been scored on the road.

"I guess to me the most important thing is it's close to a goal a game," Wayne said of the record. "That and the fact that I set the record at home in front of Edmonton fans."

The regular season behind them, the Oilers found themselves matched up against the Los Angeles Kings in the opening rounds of the Smythe Division semifinal series. Game One ended in defeat, 5–2, but the loss proved to be all the motivation Edmonton needed. They came back to embarrass the Kings 13–3 in Game Two. Three straight victories later (the opening Stanley Cup round was now the best of seven), the Oilers were on their way to the Smythe finals against the Winnipeg Jets.

The Jets played their best in each game but in the end were no match for Gretzky and his Oilers. Edmonton rode a four-game sweep and an eight-game playoff winning streak into the Campbell Conference finals.

Four wins later, the Oilers sent the Detroit Red Wings packing.

Captain Gretzky and his Oilers were back in the Stanley Cup finals. They were four wins away from banishing the painful memories of the previous spring's failure.

Standing between them and the coveted Cup were the Philadelphia Flyers. It would be a rematch of the 1985 finals.

Before the game, Wayne Gretzky had been held without a goal for five straight. In Game One, Number 99 ended this rare offensive slump with a goal in the first period and an assist to Paul Coffey for the game-winning goal in the third. Noticeably excited, Wayne later commented that the goal had taken "a lot of pressure and tension off" him. The Oilers won, 4–2.

The pressure was back on in Game Two, but again, Wayne came through. In a three-cornered passing play six minutes into overtime, he shot the puck to Paul Coffey, who sent it to Jari Kurri for the winning goal.

The Flyers rallied back to take the third game, then fell to the Oilers in Game Four. They had tried a tough double-teaming defense on Wayne, but Number 99 exhibited his usual poise and discipline, and waited for the right moment to pass the puck out of danger. The game ended 4–1 and the Oilers now had a 3-games-to-1 lead.

The Flyers weren't ready to lie down, however. They survived Game Five 4–3 and returned the series to Philadelphia. In Game Six, Flyer goaltender Ron Hextall — later named the Conn Smythe MVP — slammed the door on the Oilers 3–2.

The series stood at 3 games apiece. Not since 1971 had the Stanley Cup come down to one game to determine a champion. The tiebreaker would be played in Edmonton.

It was a Game Seven that lived up to its advance promotion. From the outset the Flyers' tight-checking style frustrated the speedy Edmonton forwards. Trailing 1–0 halfway through the second period, the Oilers managed to draw even, then pull ahead when left wing Esa Tikkanen knocked the puck away from a Flyer defenseman onto the waiting stick of Wayne Gretzky. Wayne looked up, found Jari Kurri behind the net, and passed. Kurri buried the puck and the Oilers led, 2–1.

The Oilers knew that a one-goal lead didn't mean a certain victory. They played tough defense throughout the third period, limiting Philadelphia to a mere two shots on goal. But it wasn't until Glenn Anderson plugged in a third goal with less than two and a half minutes to go that the Edmonton fans really began to celebrate.

When the buzzer sounded, the roar from the crowd was deafening. The Cup was back where everybody thought it would stay for a long time: Edmonton.

Amid the postgame euphoria, Captain Gretzky reflected.

"It was the hardest Cup we have won," he said. "I thought we played seven good games of hockey. This was by far the biggest game I've ever played. It could have been a great summer or the longest summer of my life."

To put the icing on the cake, Wayne added his eighth straight Hart Trophy (MVP) and seventh consecutive Art Ross Trophy (scoring champion). All the individual honors aside, the most important fact for Wayne was that he had brought the Oilers back to the top. His 34 points (5 goals, 29 assists) led all playoff scorers for the fifth time in six years.

But the hockey season wasn't over yet. The challenge of the Canada Cup was still ahead. For Wayne, this tournament would prove to be a turning point.

Though the 1986–87 season ended in triumph and glory for the Oilers, it had been a grueling one for Number 99. He had been playing competitive hockey for twenty years with barely a break. Physically and mentally exhausted, the twenty-six-year-old actually contemplated retirement.

The Canada Cup gave Wayne an opportunity to remember why he had been drawn to hockey in the first place. He was teamed up with a younger player who was emerging as the heir apparent to his throne: Mario Lemieux of the Pittsburgh Penguins. Playing with "Super Mario" proved to be just the revitalizing experience Wayne needed.

The 1987 Canada Cup was one of the best showcases of international hockey talent ever held. Teams from the United States, Sweden, Finland, Russia, and Canada competed in front of a worldwide audience.

In the end, co-favorites Canada and Russia matched up for the finals. Those watching the best-of-three series saw some of the greatest hockey ever played. And at the center of it all was hockey's Great One, Wayne Gretzky.

The opening game of the final was played on September 11 at the historic Montreal Forum. The crowd was treated to a terrific, end-to-end fast-paced match. The Russians squandered a 4–1 lead, allowing Canada to plug in 3 goals to tie the game. Wayne Gretzky broke a 4–4 tie with less than three minutes left to play. But the Russians fought back with a goal of their own and forced the game into overtime. Five minutes into the overtime, Russian left wing Alexander Semak scored, stunning the Canadians and their fans. Russia was now up a game in the best-of-three series.

Moving to Hamilton, Ontario, for Game Two, Team Canada rebounded with an exhilarating 6–5 victory in double overtime. The winning goal was made by Mario Lemieux, on an assist from Wayne Gretzky. But the tournament wasn't over yet.

The third and deciding match was also played in Hamilton. It was a hockey masterpiece.

The Russians jumped out quickly to a 3–0 lead. Spurred on by their hometown fans at Hamilton's Copps Coliseum, Team Canada scratched and clawed their way back with 2 goals. Then Wayne Gretzky tied it up on a key power play. From his favorite position behind the net, he waited for defenseman Larry Murphy to move in off the point. As Murphy hit the open area, Wayne fed him the puck for a quick wrist shot that tied the game.

The duo would also work together to plug in the game-winning goal. With the game tied at 5–5, Wayne led a three-on-one break with Mario Lemieux and Larry Murphy. The crowd roared as the Great One used Murphy as a decoy, then sent a perfect drop pass to Super Mario for a wicked shot. With a decisive flick of his stick, Mario sent the puck shooting past goalie Sergei Mylinkov into the net.

As the five-feet-eleven-inch Gretzky leaped jubilantly into the arms of the imposing six-feet-four-inch Lemieux, cameras whirred and flashbulbs popped. The dynamic duo had brought hockey glory to all of Canada as well as to themselves. For the third straight time, Wayne led the tournament in scoring with 3 goals and 18 assists for 21 points. He had assisted on all four of Mario's goals in the final series; the effort earned him Canada Cup MVP honors for the first time.

Wayne called the victory his "greatest game ever." But the celebration would be short-lived. In less than a month, Wayne and the Oilers were preparing for their Stanley Cup defense.

Chapter Fifteen:
1987–88

Changes

Things began to change in Edmonton prior to the 1987–88 season. The Oilers owner, Peter Pocklington, was suffering financial troubles.

The Edmonton Oilers of the 1980s were similar to the National Football League's Green Bay Packers in the 1960s: a small-town team that was extremely successful, beloved by their hometown fans. The major difference was that the Packers were, and have remained, city owned. Although Edmonton was no less proud of Wayne Gretzky and the Stanley Cup champion Oilers, financial problems for owner Peter Pocklington ultimately meant financial problems for the Oilers. Though his team had been wildly successful, in the end he simply couldn't afford to keep the star players together.

The first to go was Paul Coffey, traded to

Pittsburgh. Then a contract problem sent goalie Andy Moog, half of the Oilers' impenetrable tandem of netminders, to the Canadian national team. Finally, the highly skilled defenseman Reijo Ruotsalainen accepted a better offer from his native Finland.

It was a difficult year for Wayne and the remaining members of the team. For the first time, tension had also developed between Glenn Sather and Captain Wayne Gretzky regarding a new contract. The overall atmosphere was not pleasant.

But despite all the problems surrounding the team off the ice, on the ice the Oilers remained formidable. Kevin Lowe stepped into Paul Coffey's place and had his best season. Left wing Craig Simpson, acquired in the Coffey trade from Pittsburgh, scored 43 goals. Goalie Grant Fuhr's 40 wins and 4 shutouts led the NHL and earned him a place on the All-Star team as well as his first Vezina Trophy.

The Oilers finished the season with the league's third-best record with 44 wins, 25 losses, and 11 ties. Their 99 points placed them 6 points behind Calgary in the Smythe Division, ending their six-year reign as division champions.

For Wayne personally, it was a year of both highs and lows. On the positive side Wayne got his 1,000th career assist in November, becoming only the second player to reach that milestone. Then on March 1, 1988, he broke Gordie Howe's assist record with number 1,050 on a goal by Jari Kurri. It had taken him just 687 games to become the all-time leader. His boyhood idol Howe had needed 1,086 games.

On the downside, Wayne suffered his first significant injury. In a game with Philadelphia, he was sandwich-checked by two Flyer defenders and tore the cartilage in his knee. Although he didn't need surgery, he was sidelined for sixteen games, exactly one-fifth of the schedule. While it proved a good chance to rest his exhausted body at the close of the regular season, he watched Mario Lemieux walk off with first place in points and goals, the Art Ross MVP award, and the coveted first-team center spot on the All-Stars.

Amazingly enough, however, Lemieux's Penguins were not eligible for the Stanley Cup playoffs. Instead, the Oilers met the Winnipeg Jets in the Smythe Division Conference. They defeated them easily, 4 games to 1, and advanced to the semifinals.

There they found their old rivals, the Calgary Flames, waiting.

The Oilers skated to two victories on the Calgary home ice. Wayne scored a key breakaway goal in the first game, then blasted a shorthanded overtime shot in the second. They returned to Edmonton. Two games later, the Flames were done. The Oilers chalked up a 4-game sweep.

Next up was the Detroit Red Wings. Five games later, Edmonton had advanced to the Stanley Cup finals for the fifth time in six years.

This year, the Oilers faced a new challenger: the Boston Bruins. The Bruins had competed often in the pre-Cup conferences, but had always been defeated before reaching the finals. This year, they went all the way.

Led by their great defenseman, Ray Bourque, power forward Cam Neely, and netminder Reggie Lemelin, the Bruins came into the finals on a roll. But they proved to be no match for the defending Cup champions.

Like the New York Islanders years before, the Oilers drew on their playoff toughness and experience. They swept the first three games, two before their home crowd in Edmonton and the third in Boston. Strange as it may seem, the controversies of the 1987–88 season left the players actually looking forward to winning the Cup in Boston. But a power outage at the aging Boston Garden shifted Game Four back to Edmonton's Northlands Coliseum.

At first, it was a tight game. Then, with the score tied at 2–2, the Oilers took control with one of their classic offensive explosions, striking 3 unanswered goals on former Edmonton goalie Andy Moog. The game ended with a 6–3 victory.

Gretzky's 12 goals, 31 assists, and outstanding leadership earned him his second Conn Smythe Trophy as playoff MVP.

Amid another rousing postgame celebration Wayne called everyone together for a team picture. That team included many new players, a fact that led Captain Gretzky to comment, "What's great now is seeing the guys' faces who haven't won it before."

The players may have changed but the results were the same. Captain Wayne Gretzky and his Stanley Cup champion Oilers had proved again to be the most talented team in the NHL. They were a close-knit group of team members and their families; the parents of many players became lifelong friends. Playing in a small city, the team had developed a special bond with their legion of fans. As Wayne said that night, "Tonight we stand here with four Cups in five years and it just gets better every year."

All that was about to change.

Chapter Sixteen:
1988–89

From Oiler to King

The aftermath of the Oilers' 1988 Stanley Cup championship was an emotional roller coaster for hockey's greatest player.

On July 16, 1988, he married Janet Jones, a beautiful blond American actress. Wayne had met Janet some seven years earlier while taping a television show. The wedding at St. Joseph's Cathedral Basilica in Edmonton was billed by the media as "Canada's Royal Wedding," referring to the 1981 British royal wedding of Prince Charles and Lady Diana.

The Edmonton fire department, decked out in dress reds, lined the steps leading into the church. There were seven hundred invited guests. A crowd of ten thousand gathered outside the church for a glimpse of the couple. Television personality Alan

Thicke served as master of ceremonies for the lavish reception. Then Wayne and his new bride were off to Los Angeles for their honeymoon.

Wayne couldn't have been happier. But all was not well.

A few hours after the Oilers had won the Cup, Wayne's father, Walt, heard rumors that Wayne might be traded. As stunning as it sounded, Wayne had to believe deep down that this could happen. Peter Pocklington's other business ventures continued to slide. He needed cash if he was going to keep the Oilers. Unloading Wayne's hefty personal services contract would be a significant saving.

There were four teams in the running for Wayne: the Detroit Red Wings, the New York Rangers, the Vancouver Canucks, and the Los Angeles Kings. While on honeymoon with Janet, Wayne got a call from Bruce McNall, the owner of the Los Angeles Kings.

Wayne and Bruce got along well, but Wayne was not fully sold on the Kings. Los Angeles had been a poor team for a number of years and Wayne had to consider what it would mean to be thrust into the role of "franchise savior." In the end, he decided to accept it as a new challenge.

A basic deal was offered. In exchange for Wayne and forwards Marty McSorley and Mike Krushelnyski, the Oilers would receive young forwards Jimmy Carsen and Martin Gelinas from the Kings, along with three future number one draft choices and $15 million. It was an offer Pocklington couldn't refuse.

The trade was announced on August 9, 1988. A tearful Wayne Gretzky faced his Edmonton fans and spoke from the heart to the teammates, coaches, and other Oiler associates he had grown up with over the past nine years.

The shock waves were felt across the NHL. The *Edmonton Journal* ran its biggest headline since World War II ended: "Gretzky Gone." The *Edmonton Sun* listed stories on practically every page. Many in Canada cried that their national treasure had been stolen by the Americans, in particular by owner McNall — the horse owner and collector of rare art, coins, and baseball cards now had hockey's greatest player as well.

Wayne experienced culture shock in moving to

L.A. After years of sharing apartments with teammates like Kevin Lowe, he was married and living in a mansion in suburban Encino. His new home included six bedrooms, a swimming pool, and servants. But once he got used to his surroundings, he found the city had many advantages. For one, he was no longer the only celebrity in town. He could get lost among the hordes of stars that populated Los Angeles. He could socialize with close friends and fellow Canadians Alan Thicke, Michael J. Fox, and John Candy without constantly being mobbed.

The trade proved to be beneficial for the Kings, too. Season ticket sales skyrocketed from four thousand to over thirteen thousand. On opening night, Roy Orbison sang the national anthem before a crowd that had sold out even though the Dodgers were playing in the World Series that same night.

Coach Rob Ftorek, who had taken over halfway through the previous season, had turned a team comfortable with losing into a team fighting to win. Wearing his old number but a new uniform, Wayne was ready to join in the battle against the Detroit Red Wings.

He didn't waste any time proving that he could adjust to his new team's method of play. With the Kings enjoying a five-on-three two-man power play advantage, winger Dave Taylor fed Wayne a perfect pass just to the right of Red Wing Greg Stefan. Wayne caught the puck on his stick and quickly dished it by the goalie. Score! His first shot on net found its mark. He finished the night with 3 assists, helping the Kings to their first victory of the season.

On October 19, 1988, Wayne found himself back in Edmonton for a game against the Oilers. He dreaded the visit. If L.A. won, he would have beaten some of his best friends. If L.A. lost, the Kings and their owner would appear to have paid too high a price for their newest player. Either way, Number 99 felt he would come up the loser.

Oilers coach Glen Sather didn't say a word to Wayne when he arrived at the rink. It was to be strictly business. Owner Peter Pocklington wanted Wayne to pose for a friendly picture with him but, following Sather's lead, Wayne refused.

When he entered the rink from the visitors' end, Wayne was unsure of what to expect. To his amazement, the fans greeted him with a thunderous ovation. Even though he no longer played for the Oilers, he was still the man who had built their beloved team into what it was. They would not soon forget the four Stanley Cups Gretzky's expertise had helped earn.

It was an emotionally and physically charged game. Wayne got 2 assists — and a bad bruise on a check from his old friend Mark Messier. The Kings lost 8–6 and Wayne lost his inhibitions about playing against his former teammates. He wasn't an Oiler anymore.

As the 1988 season unfolded, the Kings quickly earned a reputation as a "run 'n' gun" free-skating, wide open offensive machine. Fans were flocking to the Great Western Forum. On the road, the team played to one sellout crowd after another, something they had failed to do even once the season before.

By the All-Star break, the Kings had achieved by far their best ever first-half-of-the-season record: 24-15-1. Reunited with Jari Kurri for the game in Edmonton, Wayne picked up a goal and 2 assists. He was once again honored with the MVP award.

The team slumped a bit in the second half of the

season (18-16-6), but approached the playoffs in good position overall. A combination of veterans like Dave Taylor and Bernie Nicholls and third-year player Luc Robitaille vaulted the Kings to the top position in total goals in the NHL with 370. In one of the greatest turnarounds in hockey history, they placed second in the Smythe Division with 12 more victories and 23 more points than in the previous season.

Though Wayne finished second to Mario Lemieux in the scoring race, his 114 assists led the league for the tenth consecutive year. Among his 54 goals was the 600th of his career. His injuries now completely healed, he played in 78 of 80 regular-season games.

The Great One was overwhelmed by emotions as the 1989 playoffs began. The Kings' first opponent was a team of familiar foes: the Oilers.

In Game One, goalie Grant Fuhr stopped Wayne cold. Wayne now knew what it had been like for opposing forwards to go against Fuhr when the money was on the line. Edmonton prevailed 4–3 that night, but the Kings evened it up in the second game. Back in Edmonton, Mark Messier led the Oilers to victory with 3 goals and 4 assists in Games Three and

Four. Down 3 games to 1, the Kings rallied back in the next 2 games to tie the series.

Los Angeles had gone hockey mad. The Magic Johnson–Laker fans had discovered the Great Western Forum's other winter resident: Wayne Gretzky and his Kings. They flocked to the stadium for the final game of the series.

Fifty-two seconds into the deciding match, Wayne scored against his old teammate Grant Fuhr. The game turned into a frantic end-to-end battle between the two offensively charged teams. First Jari Kurri tied the game, then Chris Kontos of the Kings upped the score another notch. Edmonton's Craig Simpson answered and brought the score even again. High-scoring Kings center Bernie Nicholls took the lead back, but Oilers defenseman Kevin Lowe added one of his own. The score read 3–3.

But that was as high a score as the Oilers could get. Bernie Nicholls chalked up another goal on a 5-on-3 power play, then defenseman Dale DeGray sweetened the lead with yet another. In the final minute and a half, Wayne Gretzky iced the game with an empty-net tally.

Final score: 6–3. The Forum erupted. The series

was over — and with the game behind them, Wayne and his former teammates could finally talk as friends.

The Smythe Division final catchup with Calgary was almost anticlimactic. The Flames swept the Kings in four straight games. Despite its disappointing conclusion, the year had been a positive one for Los Angeles. With Wayne Gretzky, the Kings had moved up two spots in the division and improved by 23 points overall. Wayne himself had accepted his ninth Hart Trophy.

The transition from Canada to L.A. had been challenging, but now his future seemed bright, both on the rink and off. In addition to having a tremendous first year, Wayne found himself playing a new role — that of father to his first child, Paulina. He took to fatherhood with great joy. Two years later, his and Janet's second child, Tyler, was born, followed by Trevor two years after that. From all indications, Wayne was content to settle down in southern California.

Then, in August of 1989, Wayne received a request to return to the town of Edmonton for a ceremony unveiling a statue outside of the Northlands

Coliseum. Since many of his former Oilers team-mates were participating, he agreed to attend. Nothing he experienced in hockey had prepared him for what happened there.

The building was sold out. A huge parade was organized. The statue itself was a six-foot-high bronze of Wayne in his Oilers uniform holding the Stanley Cup overhead.

When called upon to speak, Wayne had tears in his eyes. He spoke of his greatest years, the lifelong friends and memories. He mentioned his own boyhood idol, Gordie Howe, and the long-ago night he met him at the sports banquet in Brantford. As he talked, one thing became clear: Wayne Gretzky might live and play in L.A., but his home would always be in Edmonton.

Chapter Seventeen:

1989–94

Shattering All Records

Wayne's second season in Los Angeles was one of great personal triumph. Despite a back injury (an ominous sign of a future ailment) that sidelined him for the last five games of the regular season, he regained the scoring title for the first time in three years, posting 40 goals and 102 assists, for 142 points.

Early in the season, on October 15, 1989, at Edmonton, Wayne was on the threshold of breaking hockey's all-time scoring record. The mark of 1,850 points had been established by Wayne's idol, Gordie Howe. As he neared the mark Wayne felt a little uncomfortable. Was he worthy to hold this record? Howe had been among the top five league scorers for twenty straight years. At forty-eight he had been named MVP of the now defunct WHA.

He was still Wayne's all-time hockey hero. Wayne almost wished he could just stop at 1,850 and share the record. He thought it might be nice to see Number 9 and Number 99 on the same line in the record book.

Gordie and his wife, Colleen, were in Edmonton to see Wayne set the record in a game against the Oilers. Walt and Phyllis Gretzky were also there, as was Wayne's wife, Janet.

With an early assist, the Great One drew even with his idol. For much of the rest of the game, though, it looked as though the record would stay that way. The Oilers' tenacious defensive forward, Esa Tikkanen, shadowed Wayne all over the ice. Late in the third period, the Oilers led 4–3 and Wayne still trailed the record by one.

There was under a minute remaining when L.A.'s Steve Duchesne intercepted a clearing pass by Edmonton defenseman Kevin Lowe. Gretzky headed to the net. He picked up the puck off the knee of teammate Dave Taylor, then lifted a backhand shot high over Edmonton goalie Bill Ranford. Score!

Wayne leaped into the arms of Kings defenseman Larry Robinson. The Northlands Coliseum crowd erupted. It didn't matter what jersey Wayne was wearing — he was their hometown hero once again.

The game stopped as Walt, Janet, Bruce McNall, and Gordie Howe and his wife rushed out on the ice to congratulate Number 99. After order was restored and the game resumed, a fired-up Wayne Gretzky scored yet another goal in overtime on a backhander. The Kings took the game, 5–4.

The Kings went on to finish fourth in the Smythe Division. While Wayne battled his back woes, Los Angeles upset Calgary in seven games. Then the Oilers gained a measure of revenge for the previous year by sweeping Los Angeles four games to none. Wayne's second season in L.A. ended.

Wayne showed no signs of slowing down in the 1990–91 season. His 41 goals and 122 assists for 163 points were good enough for his ninth Art Ross Trophy in eleven years. He broke his own assist scoring record with a 23-game streak. Wayne also picked up his 2,000th point and became the fourth player in history to record 700 goals. Best of all, the back problems of the previous year didn't recur.

Most important, the Kings, under new coach Tom Webster, surged to the Smythe Division title with

102 points, third best in the league overall. Expectations were high as the playoffs approached.

The Kings dropped two of their first three playoff matches to the underdog Vancouver Canucks before turning the series around with three straight wins. For the third year in a row Wayne would battle his former team in a playoff series.

Edmonton had finished some 22 points behind Los Angeles in the regular season. But this was the playoff season and the Oilers were the defending Stanley Cup champions. They had won a Cup without the Great One. Could Wayne lead Los Angeles to hockey's Holy Grail?

The series' first three games all went to overtime. Luc Robitaille won the first game for L.A., but Edmonton took the next two, then added a third and fourth victory to oust Los Angeles from the contest. Wayne was bitterly disappointed. He had played his hardest, but not even his 15 points in 12 playoff games had been enough.

Los Angeles didn't approach the lofty heights of its previous regular season in 1991–92. The team's 84 points positioned it in second place. Wayne led the league in assists for the twelfth time with 90, but his goal total slipped to a career low of 31. A disappointing, abrupt playoff season and accompanying subpar effort by Wayne had hockey fans wondering if this could be the end of the line for 99.

They seemed to receive their answer in the 1992 off-season. Wayne's amazing stretch of injury-free professional hockey came to an end.

Arriving at training camp in top shape, anxious to erase the memory of the previous year's quick playoff exit, Wayne began to experience excruciating chest pain. He was forced to stay in the hospital for a week. The injury was diagnosed as a herniated thoracic disk. It was a condition that had permanently sidelined other athletes.

For two months he endured the pain. When treatments began to reduce the disk swelling, he made an announcement: he was determined to beat the odds and play again.

Wayne's whole life had been hockey. In the end, the thought of not playing frightened him more than the threat of further injury.

Wayne made his triumphant return to a sold-out Great Western Forum on January 6, 1993. He had missed 39 games, but the painful injury was finally a memory. In his first game back he picked up 2 assists. In the second, he scored 2 goals. The Great One had indeed returned.

Playing in the season's remaining 45 games, Wayne tallied an amazing 65 points with 16 goals and 49 assists. Forty-six of his points came in his last 27 matches. With Wayne back in the lineup, the Kings won 11 games, tied 6, and lost only 3. They finished the regular season third in the Smythe Division with 84 points. Playoff expectations were low — but the Kings weren't about to give up yet.

In the opening round Los Angeles dispatched second-place Calgary 4 games to 2. Then they treated the Vancouver Canucks to a similar defeat in the Smythe Division final, winning in six games. Suddenly the success-starved city of Los Angeles was excited about hockey again.

Advancing to the conference finals for the first time since 1989, Wayne could see the second of his two long-term goals in focus. When traded to L.A. in 1988 he first wanted to sell southern California on hockey. That he had accomplished. The second goal was to bring the Stanley Cup to Los Angeles. Now that too had become a possibility.

The playoffs had revitalized Wayne Gretzky. He was playing his best hockey since the September 1991 Canada Cup. The entire hockey world breathed a sigh of relief. The Great One would skate on.

Averaging close to 2 points per game, Wayne looked forward to the Campbell Conference finals. The opponent would be the Toronto Maple Leafs.

An exhilarating seven-game series followed. Trailing 3 games to 2, Wayne's power play goal in the sixth-game overtime sent the Great Western Forum crowd into a frenzy.

Game Seven was to be played in Toronto. Number 99 had saved his best for last.

Wayne dominated the game, leading the Kings to a 5–4 victory with 3 goals and 1 assist. The last goal was a crucial all-or-nothing tiebreaker. The Great One carried the puck deep into the Toronto zone with defenseman Todd Gill covering him the entire way. Wayne swung to his favorite place behind the net, managed to free his stick from Gill's tight defense, and directed the puck to the front of the net. It skipped off the back of a Toronto defender's skate and slipped into the goal. Score! Though the Maple

Leafs would score again before the game ended, victory went to L.A.

It had taken five years for Gretzky's Oilers to win the Stanley Cup in Edmonton. It was Wayne's fifth year in Los Angeles. The Kings would play for the Stanley Cup for the first time.

"I don't think I've ever had as much personal satisfaction," Gretzky commented after leading his team to their first finals ever. The fact that Game Seven had been played just down the road from Brantford had made it all the sweeter.

The Kings invaded Montreal and won the opening Game. Game Two was lost when Montreal's coach accused Los Angeles defenseman Marty McSorley of playing with an illegally curved stick. The accusation proved well-founded, and Montreal converted the penalty that followed into a game-winning goal. The next two games were played in Los Angeles before a throng of celebrities that included former President Ronald Reagan and his wife, Nancy. The Canadiens won both in thrilling overtime battles.

Returning to Montreal for the fifth game, the Canadiens and their magnificent goalie Patrick Roy all but shut out Gretzky and the Kings' potent offense. Shadowed the entire night, Wayne was unable to get his usual high caliber of offensive play up to speed.

At the end of the fifth game, the scoreboard read 4–1. Montreal walked away with their twenty-fourth Stanley Cup. The Kings' dreams were shattered.

Though for the sixth time in his career he led all playoff scorers with 15 goals and 25 assists for 40 points, a dejected Wayne Gretzky spoke openly about retirement. Yet even as he said the words in the Kings' postgame locker room, he knew he would return. One record remained to be broken.

It took a good portion of the 1993–94 season, but Wayne accomplished what he had set out to do. On March 23, 1994, at the Great Western Forum in Los Angeles, nearing the end of a season in which he would win his tenth scoring title, he became the NHL's all-time goal scorer. The mark of 801 had been set by Gordie Howe and had stood for fourteen years. Howe had played 1,767 games over twenty-six seasons. The Great One, with all due respect to his hero, had needed just 1,117 games over fifteen seasons to better the mark.

At 14:47 of the second period, Wayne connected on a wrist shot from the base of the left circle. Assisting on the goal was his long-time teammate from his Edmonton days, Marty McSorley. The game between the Kings and Vancouver Canucks was held up for ten minutes for a ceremony at center ice to honor the new record. As always, Wayne's father and mother were on hand to share the moment along with his wife, Janet.

"It's the greatest game in the world," the Great One told the crowd. "And I feel great that I play in the NHL."

Wayne Gretzky is still going strong. When he does retire he can walk away secure in the knowledge that no athlete has ever dominated a major team sport the way he has. He owns every major National Hockey League scoring record, sixty-one in all. He has been his own competition over the course of his career.

He is responsible for spreading the popularity of the game throughout the world. Yet he has remained humble and giving through it all, raising millions for charities such as the Canadian National

Institute for the Blind with his annual softball and tennis tournaments.

Skating in his familiar hunched-over style, he never forgot the long-ago lessons his father taught him on the Nith River at his grandparents' farm and the Wally Coliseum in his backyard: "Let the puck do the work . . . you can't outskate it"; "Look for the open ice between the defensemen and the forwards"; "Go where the puck is going to be, not where it's been."

A *USA Today* poll once rated Wayne Gretzky as the fourth-ranked athlete of the twentieth century. He trailed only Muhammad Ali, Babe Ruth, and Jim Thorpe. Like these sportsmen, Wayne has done much more than capture unbeatable records — he has given us a glimpse of greatness.

Epilogue:
1995–96

The Kings' 1993 appearance in the Stanley Cup finals turned out to be the high-water mark of the Great One's tenure in Los Angeles.

The Kings slumped badly the following year and Wayne's hopes of bringing the Stanley Cup to southern California faded. Then rumors of a Gretzky trade started circulating throughout the hockey world.

On February 28, 1996, the rumors became a reality. The St. Louis Blues gave up three prospects and two draft choices to bring Number 99 to their team. But St. Louis was not to be the Great One's home for long. On July 22, 1996, a mere five months later, he announced that he had agreed to a two-year, $8 million contract with the New York Rangers.

His reasons for switching seemed to take some

people by surprise. Many star players make a change because they see an opportunity to earn more money. But money is not what the Great One is about. In fact, the contract pays him nearly $2.5 million less per year than he made in the 1995–96 season with the Kings and Blues.

"It was a tough decision," Wayne told reporters at a press conference. "I guess probably what tipped the scale was the chance to play with Mark [Messier] and the opportunity to get a chance to play with a team that is really focused on trying to win a championship."

Only time will tell whether Wayne Gretzky can help the Rangers win another Stanley Cup or whether the dynamic duo of Gretzky and Messier that sparked the Edmondton Oilers nine years ago can recapture the rhythm that made them unstoppable. But one thing is for sure: the greatest hockey player in history shows no signs of slowing down.

Matt Christopher

Michael Jordan

Steve Young

Wayne Gretzky

Grant Hill